Overcomers

30 Stories of Triumph from the Bible

⟵ *«»* ⟶

David Ettinger

CROSSLINK
PUBLISHING

Overcomers:30 Stories of Triumph from the Bible

CrossLink Publishing
www.crosslinkpublishing.com

Copyright, © 2015 David Ettinger

All rights reserved. No part of this book may be reproduced in any form, except for brief quotations in reviews, without the written permission of the author.

Printed in the United States of America. All rights reserved under International Copyright Law.

ISBN 978-1-63357-020-7

Library of Congress Control Number: 2015930231

Scripture quotations are taken from THE HOLY BIBLE, NEW INTERNATIONAL VERSION®, NIV® Copyright © 1973, 1978, 1984, 2011 by Biblica, Inc.™ Used by permission. All rights reserved worldwide.

Contents

←«»→

About This Collection v
A Word from the Author ix

Adam and Eve: Overcoming the Fall 1
Sarah: Overcoming Old Age 11
Leah: Overcoming Lovelessness 21
Joseph: Overcoming Treachery 31
Moses: Overcoming Shortcomings 41
Naomi: Overcoming Tragedy 51
Hannah: Overcoming Misery 61
Abigail: Overcoming Marital Distress 71
Bathsheba: Overcoming Blatant Sin 81
Widow of Zarephath: Overcoming Poverty 91
Josiah: Overcoming an Evil Lineage 99
Daniel: Overcoming Separation 107
Nehemiah: Overcoming Opposition 115
Job: Overcoming Great Suffering 125
Hosea: Overcoming an Adulteress Marriage 133
Elizabeth: Overcoming Hopelessness 143

Peter: Overcoming Failure 153

Matthew: Overcoming an Evil Past 161

Thomas: Overcoming Doubt 171

Woman at the Well: Overcoming Immorality 179

Martha: Overcoming Disappointment 187

The Woman Who Washed Jesus' Feet: Overcoming Shame 197

Mary Magdalene: Overcoming Worthlessness 207

Nicodemus: Overcoming Cultural Pressure 215

The Greek Woman: Overcoming Barriers 225

Thief on the Cross: Overcoming Eternal Judgment 235

Paul: Overcoming Hatred 245

Mark: Overcoming Cowardice 255

The Philippian Jailer: Overcoming Fear 265

Timothy: Overcoming Timidity 275

About This Collection

←❮❯→

Many years ago, King Solomon wrote: "Of making many books there is no end" (Ecclesiastes 12:12). If that was true in centuries gone by, how much more is it true today? Obviously, it is impossible to read even a small fraction of the books being published, even if the choices were restricted to Christian publications. It is apparent then that selectivity in reading material is required. *Overcomers: 30 Stories of Triumph from the Bible* should be on the list of books highly worth reading. Its author, David Ettinger, spent almost two decades as a newspaper journalist, much of that as a sportswriter, and his diversity of skills is seen in the range of his writing: from sports to Bible doctrine and just about everything in between.

He unites his various writing influences—the fluidity and color of his sportswriting days and the solemnity of his fiction and Bible doctrine writing—to give us a collection of works that will impact and move you to the deepest recesses of your soul.

In *Overcomers: 30 Stories of Triumph from the Bible*, David writes of familiar as well as lesser-known Bible personalities. Some were on the stage of the Old Testament; others lived their parts after the curtain rose for the New Testament. Some were men, and some were women; some were kings, and some were commoners. All, however, left their stories of encouragement behind for you and me that we might draw strength and hope from them.

The author, after careful biblical research and using a sanctified imagination, takes his reader one step beyond the conspicuous and gives to his carefully chosen biblical personalities bone and sinew, flesh and blood—all the "stuff" of which humanity is made. There is no fiction here.

It is impossible to read *Overcomers: 30 Stories of Triumph from the Bible* without experiencing all of the emotions and pathos its biblical personalities experienced. This is a volume for men and women; it is tender, yet it is strong. It will touch the heart. It will activate the will.

Whether it is the hopelessness and despair of Leah, the wife of Jacob, living a life of lovelessness; the fear faced by Moses at the prospect of leading a nation; the grief of Peter after he denied His Lord three times; the perceived worthlessness of Mary Magdalene, who was possessed by seven demons; or the account of the other twenty-six personalities—their triumph of faith will stand like rays of sunlight in the midst of the darkness.

These very personal and emotional accounts will bring you comfort, insight, and blessing. But more than this, a small section following each account will bring you practical advice regarding your own struggles and challenges.

I now invite you to begin your journey through *Overcomers: 30 Stories of Triumph from the Bible* and wish you "Godspeed" on the trip. It will be an adventure well worth the effort.

Marvin J. Rosenthal

Executive Director, Zion's Hope, Inc.

A Word from the Author

←«»→

Since coming to faith in Christ in 1986, I have read through the entire Bible twice yearly. The reason for this is my passion for the Word of God. To me, the Bible is the greatest book ever written in that it:

- Reveals God's perfect will.
- Makes plain the way to eternal salvation.
- Provides insightful lessons on how to live.
- Unflinchingly declares what is right and wrong.
- Presents imperfect men and women in their best and worst moments.
- Gives its readers an ideal to strive for.
- Touches the spirt, intellect, and emotion like no other volume can even approach.

The Bible has done all of this for me. While its words cause my spirit to soar and satisfy the inquiries of my intellect, the Bible touches my emotions as no other. In fact, I often find myself a participant in particular portions. For instance, though I have read the account more than fifty times, I always feel like yelling out, "No, don't do it!" whenever David sends for Bathsheba, as if my feeble warning could actually prevent the event from occurring.

It is this level of emotion that inspired me to write *Overcomers: 30 Stories of Triumph from the Bible*. The people of the Bible are real, and writing about them demands the exploration of the very real, genuine, and profound emotions of joy, fear, sadness, anger, misery, distress, and triumph they experience. Trying to put myself in the head of the personality about whom I am writing, I have treated each chapter of this book in "novel-like" fashion. In other words, each account reads as fiction, with inner thought, dialogue, and a sanctified envisioning of how events may have played out. Some believe this is akin to "adding to" or "subtracting from" Holy Scriptures, but I assure you this is not the case. It is unlikely that someone who has pored over the Scriptures more than fifty times out of love, reverence, and fascination would do anything to "harm" the precious Word of God in any way.

Rather, I have written about the individuals as the Scriptures present them. In so doing, I have considered how some of these events *may have* played themselves out *within their biblical context*. It is my hope that the reader will come to appreciate Bible personalities for the very real people they are, and be able to empathize with them in a much more intimate way. In many instances, the reader will discover amazing similarities with a certain biblical personality. In other words, Leah, Naomi, and Mary are not merely characters in a book, but real women with challenges just like you. Likewise, what would you have done if you were in the shoes of Joseph, Moses, and Thomas? Chances are, you *have* been in their shoes, only the circumstances and timeframe were different.

So, please, enjoy the novel-like aspects of this engaging devotional—as well as the very practical "counsel" section—and may God use this volume to draw you ever closer to Him.

David Ettinger
Orlando, Florida, 2015

Adam and Eve
Overcoming the Fall

←❝❞→

Eve could not take her eyes off the mighty angels who dutifully stood slashing their flaming swords back and forth.

"What is the logic in this, Eve?" Adam asked impatiently. "It does no good."

"I am sorry, my husband," she replied quietly. "I am having so much trouble tearing myself away from this place. After all, it was our home."

"Standing here lamenting will only make the matter worse, Eve. Why prolong the torment?"

With that, Adam began to walk away from the Garden of Eden, which had been sealed to them forever; the powerful cherubs assured that humanity's first couple would never enter again.

Eve looked back and noticed that Adam was already some distance away. Walking ahead of her in a huff, as he was now doing, was something he never even considered before this day.

This terrible, awful day. Before it, things were different. So different. Wonderfully different.

But not anymore.

Eve turned back to the gates of Eden and looked beyond the angels for one final glance at the garden. She fought back tears as she did so, then resolutely turned and began to follow Adam. She wanted to catch up to him and take his hand, but thought it wise to allow him time to meditate. She would do the same.

"Oh, Lord," she said sorrowfully, "this horrible day. How I so regret it. It tortures my soul."

Fearful of being overcome by grief to the point of incapacity, Eve set her mind on her and Adam's early days in the garden long before the darkness set in.

How she and Adam loved exploring their wondrous home, the creative powers of God holding joyous discoveries everywhere they looked. Every tree was stately. Every plant was spectacular. Every creature was magnificent.

And the sky...oh, the sky. How Eve loved lying in Adam's embrace every night, gazing up at that star-filled black canopy, trying to count each celestial body.

"Surely you know, Eve," Adam said laughing, "how futile this all is."

"What is futile, my dear?"

"These stars that you have been trying to number all look alike. You have no hope of counting them."

"But I am already up to five hundred."

"Yes, my love, but you have counted the same stars over and over. You have no way of keeping track of which ones you have counted and which ones you have not. It is an impossible task."

Eve knew that, of course, but loved listening as Adam tried to correct her perceived silliness with his sage advice. It was a game they played, and they loved engaging in it.

During the days, the blessed couple enjoyed walking hand in hand through the garden, communing with God and visually feasting on this paradise of spectacular grandeur He had placed them in. Every day offered something new for them to see and discover, and they delighted with each new revelation.

However, there was a distraction, and it was a notable one. There was that tree in the middle of the garden, the tree of the knowledge of good and evil. Rising majestically from the ground, the tree was one of mystery and intrigue. Indeed, God had told them, "You are free to eat from any tree in the garden; but you must not eat from the tree of the knowledge of good and evil, for when you eat of it you will surely die."[1]

Adam and Eve never contemplated questioning God's will on this matter; if He said not to eat from it, that settled it. Over time, however, Eve would begin to wonder.

"Husband, why would God tell us not to eat from this one tree when we can eat from all the others?"

---

[1] Genesis 3:16–17

"I am not sure, but I have sometimes asked myself this same question."

The acknowledgement surprised Eve. "Really, my husband?" she asked expectedly.

Adam looked at her, his brow scrunched in uncertainty. "But perhaps, my love, it is best to not speak of it."

"Yes, my husband, you are right."

But Eve's fascination of the tree—specifically, God's directive not to eat from it—became an obsession. Every time she walked by the tree, she could not help but stare at it, as if trying to discover its great secret. She would often catch Adam doing the same.

Then one morning, as they strolled by the tree, they caught sight of the majestic serpent as he, too, gazed upon it. They approached him.

"I am just wondering," he ventured in innocent deception, "did God really say, 'You must not eat from any tree in the garden?'"

Eve indulged him. "We may eat fruit from any tree in the garden, but God *did* say, 'You must not eat fruit from the tree that is in the middle of the garden, and you must not touch it, or you will die.'" She was not even aware that she had added in the part about not touching the tree, which was not part of God's original decree.

"You will not surely die," the serpent assured her, his voice soft, seductive, like the gentle blowing of the breeze through the luxuriantly leafy trees. "God knows that when you eat of it your eyes will be opened, and you will be like God, knowing good and evil."

As Eve gazed longingly at the irresistible fruit, she could only imagine how wonderful it would taste. After all, any fruit so pleasing to the eye *must* taste equally as pleasing. And then there was the matter of wisdom—to be like God. What promise such a notion held!

Eve could no longer resist. At once, she reached out, grabbed hold of the fruit, and bit into it. Adam watched in amazement. The juice of the wondrous delicacy filled Eve's palate with marvelous delight. She turned and handed it to Adam, who was all too eager to eat. He, too, savored the glorious goodness of the fruit's content. Oh, how wonderful it tasted! No fruit in the garden could match it!

Then, suddenly, something happened. Adam dropped the fruit, and he and Eve looked at each other in horror. Their gaze, at first, was directed at each other's eyes, but then they began to scan one another from top to bottom.

Each instinctively covered themselves with their hands. They quickly turned from each other and ran in different directions, their hearts racing, their minds and souls in wretched disarray.

What had happened?

An hour later, they returned to the same place. They both had the same idea: to sew fig leaves together as coverings for their nakedness. They looked again at each other and trembled.

God called to them, and they tried to hide. But He relentlessly pursued them. He summoned the serpent and pronounced sentence on all three. The creature would be cursed above all animals. Furthermore, his offspring would wage a centuries-long war with that of the woman—and eventually be defeated. The woman would experience great pains in childbirth. To sustain himself, the man would have to toil laboriously to make the earth productive.

They would also be banished forever from their beloved home. "You may never return!" God proclaimed.

But before they were evicted, God had one more order of business. "These garments of figs you made for yourselves are unacceptable. I have provided new garments for you."

They looked and saw a pair of animal skins, which they clothed themselves in. The Lord then caused a great wind to blow, which ushered them to the entrance of the garden. They tried to resist leaving, but God drove them out. At that moment, the mighty angels appeared, frightening flaming swords barring the way back in. It was over.

—

After an hour of walking, Eve had finally caught up with Adam. "Where will we go?"

"I am not sure, Eve."

"These animal skins make walking difficult."

Adam stopped and turned to her. "I have been thinking about these garments, Eve."

"How so, my husband?"

"We have fallen in sin, and yet God did not take our lives from us. Instead, he killed an innocent creature in our place."

Eve pondered Adam's words. "That poor creature," she lamented.

"Yes," Adam concurred, "completely innocent."

"But not us," Eve said, a tear trickling down her face.

"No, not us. Yet, Eve, God has spared us. He has not abandoned us. We have lost paradise, but we have not lost God. He has made a way for us."

"But, my husband, we have disobeyed Him and have fallen. How can we overcome such a fall?"

"I am not sure, Eve, but God has given us these garments. He has saved us through the blood of an innocent creature. He is still with us, Eve. He is still with us."

Adam reached out his hand. Eve, relieved, took hold of it.

As they resumed walking together to the place God would settle them, Eve began to look around, as if searching.

"What is it, Eve?"

"Though I do not see Him, I feel Him walking with us. Do you feel it, too, my husband?"

"I do, dear wife. He walks with us as surely as we walk with each other."

Adam took Eve in his arms and embraced her tightly. "We will overcome this day, my beloved Eve. God will help us to overcome."

Adam and Eve and You

The fall of Adam and Eve in the Garden of Eden was the fall of all humankind.

From the moment they ate of the forbidden fruit, sin entered the world and would forever condemn humanity to eternal punishment.

Man would forever rebel against his Creator. This is humanity's natural state.

Except for one thing: God has provided a way out... for all of us.

What about you? Have you discovered the way out of eternal punishment? Knowing that you were born into sin, how will you overcome the punishment that awaits you?

In Revelation 1:15, the apostle John writes, "To him [Jesus] who loves us and has freed us from his sins by his blood."

Jesus is the answer to overcoming eternal condemnation. If you have not accepted Jesus Christ as your Lord and Savior, then you are in danger of eternal judgment. However, this does not have to be the case. The Bible says, "That if you confess with your mouth, 'Jesus is Lord,' and believe in your heart that God raised him from the dead, you will be saved" (Romans 10:9). Acts 16:31 echoes this glorious truth: "Believe on the Lord Jesus Christ and you will be saved."

In a sense, it really is *this* simple, but there are some things you should know.

First, you must acknowledge your current condition if you have not accepted Christ. Romans 3:23 states, "all have sinned and fall short of the glory of God." Notice the word *all*. People—*all* people—are born sinners, and that includes you. There are no exceptions.

Second, as a born sinner, you are subject to spiritual death—eternal separation from God: "For the wages of sin is death..." (Romans 6:23a). In this instance, sin refers to the rejection of Jesus Christ as your savior and deliverer from death. He is the *only* way. However, the remainder of this verse presents a wonderful contrast:

"…but the gift of God is eternal life in Christ Jesus our Lord" (Romans 6:23b).

A third thing you must understand is that not only is Christ "Lord" (Romans 10:9), or God, but He is also the *only* way of salvation. Acts 4:12 says, "Salvation is found in *no one* else, for there is *no other* name in heaven given to men by which we must be saved" (italics added). Faith in Jesus Christ *only* will allow you to overcome your natural inheritance of eternal punishment and acquire a supernatural heritage of eternal joy in heaven with God the Father.

Yes, Adam and Eve brought sin into the world, but don't be too harsh on them. They did what you would have done if you were in their place. But God, in His abundant mercy and grace, has given you a way out—the shed blood of Jesus Christ on the cross.

Now it's your turn. Will you stubbornly accept your death sentence, or will you overcome it by the blood of Jesus?

Salvation is yours, and God longs to give it to you!

Sarah

Overcoming Old Age

←⚜→

At age ninety, Sarah was finally a mother. And at age ninety, she finally learned the meaning of joy. But the lesson was long in coming.

As she lay in bed this early morning, she sat propped up with her back to the wall and knees raised. Her one-week-old infant Isaac slept peacefully in her lap, having exhausted his energy after nursing. Sarah gently caressed the boy's soft skin, marveling at this miracle that had come from her body.

She could have remained this way all day but knew that little Isaac would eventually awake, and she would have to tend to him. For now, however, if Isaac slept for an hour, that would be fine with her. She would quietly relish the time, contentedly stroking her son's tiny head, arms, and legs.

Her musings were interrupted when the door opened and in walked Abraham, her one-hundred-year-old husband who had become a father for the second time.

"Ah, there you are," he said, lying down next to Sarah. Then he, too, assumed the same propped-up position as she, giving him the best view of the dozing child. "When I did not see you up and about, I wondered where you were."

"Your son decided to sleep in today," she said, kissing Abraham's cheek but then returning her gaze to Isaac. "In this way, he is definitely *not* like his father."

"I suppose I am not one for sleeping late but will allow Isaac some leeway. For now."

"That is correct," Sarah replied, echoing her husband's playful tone. "We will allow just one more week, and then he must begin showing initiative. Up before dawn and out to the fields."

"Hah," Abraham said, "we will have him trained."

Abraham put his arm around Sarah's shoulder and gently drew her to him, but not too close to where he could disturb the child.

"It is good to see you laugh again, Sarah. It has been a while."

With that, he kissed her on the forehead. "Well, I guess we cannot both just lounge around watching Isaac sleep," Abraham said. "I will return to the fields, and then join the two of you for lunch."

He rose and was about to leave the room.

"And do not be late!" Sarah teasingly called to him.

Abraham laughed as he shut the door behind him.

Sarah thought for a moment, then looked up.

"He is correct, Lord," she said with a contemplative look on her face. "It has been a while since I laughed. And even when I did, it was not always for the right reasons."

As Sarah thought back over the twenty-five years that led to this moment, she could not help but cringe as she considered her demeanor, her crustiness, her...faithlessness during that time. She was a woman of sixty-five when Abraham came bursting into the house one day in Ur, the beautiful city she loved. Abraham had a wild look about him, as if he had experienced something he could not explain.

"Sarah," he said looking at her, though she could sense that he was not really seeing her, "I was out in the fields today with the workers when, suddenly, I saw that one of our oxen had gotten loose. I went to retrieve him but found that he was merely nibbling on the grain, so I decided to let him chew for a while before bringing him back."

This seemed to Sarah like a rather mundane and uneventful incident to share with her, but she politely kept her peace and listened despite her husband's detachment as he spoke.

"I was just standing there watching him when, suddenly, I heard a voice."

Abraham paused, as if transporting himself back to that moment.

The mention of the voice piqued Sarah's interest.

"The voice said, 'I am the God who made the heavens and earth, and I command you...'"

Again, Abraham stopped. Sarah could tell that he wanted to get this just right.

"'Leave your country, your people, and your father's household and go to the land I will show you. I will make you into a great nation, and I will bless you; I will make your name great, and you will be a blessing. I will bless those who bless you, and whoever curses you I will curse. And all peoples on earth will be blessed through you.'"[2]

He then sat down next to Sarah on a clump of pillows that adorned the floor. Sarah had a multitude of questions she wanted to ask Abraham but could see it was not the right time.

Abraham continued, "I am not sure what you think of what I have just said, dear wife, or even if I can make sense of it all. But this I do know..."

He faced her solemnly; the detached look was replaced with one of soberness.

"This was not imagination or some symptom of sunstroke. It was real; I know it was. And, Sarah, we must obey."

Though strong-willed, Sarah believed in obedience to her husband, especially to one as levelheaded and reasonable as Abraham. If he wanted to leave their home for a foreign land, she would follow and not complain. She would support him fully.

What intrigued her more than anything Abraham said was not the fact that they would be moving, but that this God would make Abraham the father of a nation. And if he was to be the father, then she, logic dictated, would be the mother.

But I am barren, was the first thought that came to her mind.

Ten years later, Sarah turned seventy-five and realized, to her way of thinking, that God had not kept His word. The long wait for

---

[2] Genesis 12:1–3

the promised child had embittered her, her increasing age forever mocking her accursed barrenness. She had had enough!

"The Lord has kept me from having children," she icily told Abraham. "Go, sleep with my maidservant, Hagar; perhaps I can build a family through her."[3]

Abraham bowed to Sarah's demands, slept with her Egyptian slave, and became the father of his first son, Ishmael, when Abraham was eighty-six. The child—and his mother—would become misery for Sarah, a source of heartache as they were living, breathing reminders of not only her inability to have children, but also her faithlessness in conniving the unsavory plan.

But she endured. Thirteen years later, when she was eighty-nine, three men came to visit Abraham. As Sarah eavesdropped from the entrance of their tent, she heard one of them say, "I will surely return to you about this time next year, and Sarah your wife will have a son."

To Sarah, such words were nonsense.

My years are behind me, she silently laughed in derision. *After I am worn out and my master is old, will I now have this pleasure?*

The messenger then said to Abraham, "Why did Sarah laugh and say, 'Will I really have a child, now that I am old?'"

Sarah froze and her heart began racing. This was no ordinary man; how could he have detected her thoughts? She panicked.

"I did not laugh," she lied.

---

[3] Genesis 16:1–2

"Yes, you did laugh," the messenger said, leaving Sarah feeling deceitful and cynical. She wanted to run into the fields and hide among the high stalks. Instead, she was paralyzed with fear.

The messenger turned back to Abraham. "Is anything too hard for the Lord? I will return to you at the appointed time next year, and Sarah will have a son."[4]

Three months later, Sarah's sleeping womb suddenly and miraculously awoke. Nine months following that, Isaac was born. And here he was now, sleeping in wondrous serenity.

Sarah then felt something gnawing at her. There was something she needed to say. Something that should have been said already, but she just had not gotten around to it. She knew that now was the time. Securing her grip on Isaac, Sarah closed her eyes and tilted her head upward.

"Oh, Lord," she said, as joy began to overwhelm her and manifest in her tears, "You have brought me laughter. True laughter, Lord, not laughter of ridicule or disbelief. You have looked upon me graciously, though I have dishonored You."

She laughed softly, then continued, "This child you have given me, this Isaac,[5] has brought me glorious laughter, and all who hear about him will laugh with me."[6]

She opened her eyes and looked at her son, once more caressing him. "Oh, dearest Lord," she said, her soul aflame with elation and

---

[4] Genesis 18:10–15

[5] The word "Isaac" means "he laughs."

[6] Genesis 21:6

gratitude, "who would have said to Abraham that Sarah would nurse children? Yet I have borne him a son in his old age."[7]

She laughed again and looked up. "You have done this, Lord. You! Your word is true, your promises sure. Dear Lord, may I never doubt You again. And may I never lose this blessed joy You have bestowed upon me."

She looked down at the child, then back to the Lord. "You, Lord, are my greatest joy."

Sarah and You

Besides being barren, Sarah had also reached old age. Simply put, she had gotten old, and with it, her body had gone past the point of being able to produce children, even if she were not barren.

How about you? Are you getting up in years and can no longer do the things you once did? Do you feel as if you no longer matter to God, or that He has no more use for you?

If so, then like Sarah, your perspective is all wrong. Most feelings of worthlessness in old age have to do with viewpoint.

In the book of Ezra, the Israelites went into exile for seventy years. When they returned, they built a new temple for the Lord because the former one was destroyed by the Babylonians. Those who built the new facility ranged in age from young men to those in their seventies and eighties.

---

[7] Genesis 21:7

Here's the important thing to remember. Those of older age were part of the original deportation to Babylon. In other words, they had seen Solomon's glorious temple *before* it was destroyed. The younger men who built the new temple—those born in captivity— had no idea what the original temple looked like because it was already destroyed by the time they were born.

When the foundation of the new temple was completed, we are told: "All the people gave a great shout of praise to the Lord...But many of the older priests and Levites and family heads, *who had seen the former temple*, wept aloud when they saw the foundation of this temple being laid, while many others shouted for joy" (Ezra 3:11– 12, italics added).

Why were the young men shouting? They had achieved a great accomplishment. Why were the old men weeping? This "accomplishment" was puny compared to the original temple. Where the young men saw hope and victory, the old men saw inferiority and defeat. It was all about their perspective.

God answered the older men's concerns.

"The word of the LORD came through the prophet Haggai: 'Speak to...the remnant of the people.' Ask them, 'Who of you is left who saw this house in its former glory? How does it look to you now? Does it not seem to you like nothing? But...be strong, all you people of the land...and work. For I am with you" (Haggai 2:1–4).

This is the key. God is telling the young men AND the old men to keep on working. He has a plan and wants them to pursue it regardless of how they feel about it. This same truth applies to you.

You look in the mirror and see age. You wake up in the morning and feel pain. But God sees you as a vessel through which He can *still* work mightily.

God was in no way finished with Sarah or the old returning captives who helped rebuild the temple, and He is no way finished with you!

To you, old age is an end. To God, it is just the beginning. Have the white hairs on your head outnumbered the dark? Have wrinkles begun to crease your skin? It is as nothing to God. To Him, so long as you have breath, you have a purpose. He had a purpose for Sarah, and He surely has one for you!

Leah
OVERCOMING LOVELESSNESS

←❀→

That Leah was unloved by her husband Jacob was certainly no revelation. However, trying to discern the moment she finally realized that he would *never* love her was something that presented intellectual exercise.

And that was what Leah was looking for these days. What with her children all grown, and she was not really having much to do in her waning years! Of late, she had taken to wandering the desert that skirted the family's home. As she reckoned that she had less and less to do, she found herself being led more frequently to her arid sanctuary. The barrenness of the terrain offered Leah an odd consolation, a sense of camaraderie she could not attain at home. With her six sons spending their days working in the fields and her daughter serving the family's domestic needs, Leah too often found herself bored and alone.

When the loneliness became overbearing, she would sometimes entertain herself with the notion of trekking along in the brush hand in hand with her husband Jacob. But she would quickly dismiss such flights of fancy with a derisive laugh and a pointed chastisement of her own foolishness.

"This will never happen, you silly old woman."

And yet she still held on to that irrepressible hope, which really bothered her because it was so futile. As futile as the pretentious marriage she spent the majority of her life languishing in. Pretentious indeed.

Leah still remembered the day her father Laban told her that she was to become Jacob's wife. That very night!

"But, Father," Leah objected, "Jacob loves Rachel and is to marry *her* tonight."

Jacob had worked long and hard for the privilege of marrying Leah's impossibly gorgeous sister. He had fallen helplessly in love with her at a mere glimpse seven years previous and waited all this time to claim her. Tonight would be his moment.

"Do not worry about it, Leah," Laban assured her. "Tonight *you* will be Jacob's wife."

"But, Father," she tearfully pleaded, "he does not even know I exist. Compared to Rachel, I am no more than a ... rock to him."

"We will fill him with plenty of wine. He will be none the wiser."

"But, Father ..."

"That is enough, Leah! My mind is made up. There is no way I will permit Rachel to be married before you. You are my oldest daughter, and it is my duty to take care of you."

"He despises me, Father."

"He will learn to love you, Leah."

Laban was adept at making unfulfilled promises, and this would be the pinnacle of them all.

That night, as the wedding festivities for Jacob and Rachel dragged on into the late hours, Jacob, brimming with wine, proclaimed himself ready for his bride. Rachel suddenly made herself scarce as Laban's women servants quickly attended to Leah. They dressed her in heavy marriage veils and sent her marching into Jacob's marriage tent under the cover of darkness.

After consummation, Leah slept little, fearing the dawn when the first rays of light would reveal her deception. Her dread came to fruition as Jacob rolled over to kiss his beautiful Rachel, only to discover the less attractive Leah.

Jacob's face, contorted in horror, turned ashen. *Did I sleep with HER!* his countenance dreadfully declared.

Leah wept violently while, outside their tent, her furious, deceived husband vented his rage at Laban, who calmed him by promising Jacob that if he fulfilled his wedding week with Leah, he could then have Rachel.

Seven days later, Jacob married Rachel, and Leah began a life of misery as not only the wife of no account, but also of such a far-distant one as to render her nothing more than an intolerable intrusion.

Though Jacob treated her civilly, Leah knew he most definitely did not love her.

As for Rachel, she hated Leah. Well, not at first. But then Leah began producing children—many of them. And Rachel was barren.

For Leah, it was justice. God blessed her despite the cruel fate her father had sentenced her to.

When she became pregnant the first time, Leah was sure that Jacob's heart would warm toward her. At Reuben's birth, she proclaimed, "It is because the Lord has seen my misery. Surely, my husband will love me now."

He did not. Yes, Jacob *did* give her more attention, but love? No.

Leah, however, would not surrender. At the birth of her second son, Simeon, she boldly declared, "Because the Lord heard that I am not loved, he gave me this one, too."

True, but she *still* was not loved. At least by Jacob.

Upon Levi's birth, Leah asserted, "Now at last my husband will become attached to me, because I have borne him three sons."

The couple was no more attached than they were before the birth of their third son. Jacob still loved Rachel—and *only* Rachel.

Then came Leah's fourth son, Judah. "This time I will praise the Lord."

Leah was beginning to sense that multiple children had done little in her quest for Jacob's affections.

A few years passed before Leah conceived again. She regarded son number five, Issachar, as a reward for having given her servant Zilpah to Jacob to sire more sons when she believed she had gone barren.

Then came son number six, Zebulun, and she finally got it right. "God has presented me with a precious gift. This time my husband will treat me with honor, because I have borne him six sons."

And it was true. Jacob did treat Leah with respect, dignity, and honor. In fact, he even esteemed her. And when Leah gave Jacob his only daughter, Dinah, Jacob had no option but to bestow upon Leah the prestige a mother of seven deserved. But no matter how he tried, he simply could not love her.

And Leah knew it. Lovelessness. Leah felt it. She breathed it. She was shrouded in it. It was her lot. Of course, her seven children loved her, but Jacob? It was not to be. The man was hopelessly in love with her impudent, whining wisp of a sister, Rachel—even if her looks were fading ... somewhat. Even past age forty, Rachel was *still* more attractive than Leah was at eighteen.

So, when was it that Leah finally realized that Jacob would *never* love her no matter how many offspring she produced for him? The realization dawned on her when, after years of frustrated fruitlessness, Rachel finally gave Jacob a son. His name was Joseph, and Jacob showered him with love and affection that surpassed cumulatively all of what was given to Leah's seven children.

The comprehension of Jacob's inability to love her stung her frail emotions. It substantiated her meager sense of worthiness. It crushed her battered spirit. And it hurt so much. She had nothing against Joseph; he was a good boy. But he was a product of Rachel, the wife Jacob loved. The *only* wife Jacob loved. *The only one!*

As Jacob shamelessly doted on this precious fruit of Rachel's womb, Leah felt she was drifting further and further away from Jacob's sphere of consciousness. Her children were grown, and she had little purpose. Jacob did not need her anymore. She had given him six sons who made for great field hands that helped increase the family's fortunes.

But Leah? What was her role? She had no idea.

"Oh, Lord, am I to be discarded as so much refuse?" she cried out in the still of her desert retreat. "Am I never to feel the love of a husband? Is this my fate, my Lord? Is this all my life is worth?"

She fell to her knees and poured out her sorrow, her tears watering the dry ground beneath. She wept and wept, this woman of fifty-five whose gray hairs outnumbered the dark ones three times over. She unleashed her wretchedness in waves of fury and torment, not understanding why God would allow her to endure such a sterile existence of lovelessness and anguish.

"My husband hates me, Lord!" she howled.

"My sister despises me!" she bellowed.

"My children no longer need me!" she bawled.

"Who will ever love me again, Lord! Who!"

And then, in the throes of her agony, she was suddenly engulfed in a wall of peace the likes of which she had never experienced.

"Dry your tears, Leah."

The voice consumed her, penetrating the deepest recesses of her soul.

"Do you not know that it was I who have sustained and blessed you?"

Of course she knew.

"It was I who loved you from long before your birth to this very day."

Leah felt her soul begin to soar.

"There was never a time when I did not love you, and there never will be. And when your time on this earth is over, I will be waiting for you."

Still on her knees, Leah instinctively looked up. Though the sky was blue and empty, she could see the threadbare outline of a glorious sight. A pair of arms wide open, inviting, waiting, overcoming her lovelessness. God was awaiting her, His outstretched arms offering an eternity of measureless, boundless love. She would soon triumph in His everlasting embrace—warm, secure, loved...forever.

Leah and You

Lovelessness is a terrible thing. Leah endured it her entire married life.

Perhaps you, too, are experiencing it. Are you in a loveless marriage? Are you single and don't feel there is a soul in the world who cares about you? Do you have parents incapable of displaying their love? Many people find themselves in such unenviable circumstances.

However, there is a glorious silver lining to your predicament as there was to Leah's: if you belong to the Lord, you *are* loved. Period. In fact, if you are a child of God through Jesus Christ, it is impossible for you *not* to be loved!

In the Old Testament, God tells the children of Israel: "I have loved you with an everlasting love; I have drawn you with unfailing kindness" (Jeremiah 31:3).

Guess what? As God's child, the Lord is telling you the same thing. Notice the *eternality* of God's affections. Not only does this wondrous verse tell you that God *has* loved you, but also that His love is *everlasting*. Don't forget that though humans are restricted by the ravages of time, God lives outside of time. Therefore, His love is *always*. It is past, present, and future all at once. So, doing the math, you can accurately conclude that God's love is never ending. Just as there was *never* a time when God did not love Leah, so there was never a time when God did not love you.

And there never will be when He does not love you.

Are you still unsure? Then note the second part of the above verse: "I have drawn you with unfailing kindness." Who initiated this love? You? Not a chance. The Scriptures tells you that of your own volition, you do not have the capacity to love God: "We love because he first loved us" (1 John 4:19). God's love and kindness are so great that they propelled Him to reach out to you first. The reason you love God *now* is that He *first* loved you. And just like His love, the kindness He showered upon you is "unfailing." Even if the whole world hates you, God never will and *can* never hate you. His love and kindness are eternal and unfailing. His love and kindness *for you* are eternal and unfailing.

"But surely," you may be objecting, "how can God love me? I have done so many bad things. There must be something that will cause God to withdraw His love from me."

Not according to the Scriptures. Romans 8:38–39 tells you that "neither death nor life, neither angels nor demons, neither the present nor the future, nor any powers, neither height nor depth, nor anything else in all creation, will be able to separate [you] from the love of God that is in Christ Jesus our Lord."

Sadly, like Leah, you may never receive the human love you so greatly desire. But don't fret. God's heavenly love is perpetual, persistent, and permanent, and there is nothing you can do about *that*.

Nothing, that is, but to accept and bask in it!

Joseph

OVERCOMING TREACHERY

←«»→

J oseph was shaken.

And that was unusual considering that the slave-turned-assistant monarch never felt that way. He was always calm, cool, collected, and completely in control of himself. After all, he was the second-in-command to Pharaoh, the king of Egypt, and as such was the second most powerful man in this region of the world.

But now, he was not feeling all too powerful. Far from it. He found himself feeling unsure and unsettled, emotionally stretched as never before. And he hated it!

"What is happening, Lord?" he asked apprehensively, perturbed. "I need wisdom, Lord. Please."

Joseph's anxiety had hit him suddenly. An unexpected visit. Ten brothers had come to him for food. Though he had not seen them in twenty years, he recognized them instantly. To him, they were like ghosts rising from the mists of a deep and murky past.

"Why did they have to come to me, Lord? If only they would have seen one of the other officials. That would have been so much more preferable."

But these ten brothers had come to him. And they were not just any ten brothers. They were his ten brothers. These were ten siblings who had dealt with him with such vileness that even now, two decades later, he still felt the sting of their treachery lingering in his consciousness.

It was now well past midnight as he paced in the darkness of his home, pouring his heart out to God. His wife and two sons were asleep. But there would be no sleep for him that night. There was nothing for him to do but to try to make sense of it all. And then, like a fierce windstorm rising from the desert, the dark memories from years ago began swirling around him, their heinous images blowing over him in gusts of torment.

The son of Jacob's wife Rachel, Joseph was born in his father's old age—and to his favorite wife—and therefore earned a special place of endearment in his father's heart. Sadly, Jacob committed the unpardonable sin of fatherhood: loving one child far above the rest. That Joseph had ten brothers and a sister made matters even worse. But where Jacob really went astray was when he flaunted rather than concealed his partiality to Joseph—showering Rachel's firstborn with boundless affection and expensive gifts. Young Joseph thought nothing strange of such behavior and had no clue of the rage that burned in his brothers' souls. He never paid much attention to their taunts and insults, thinking of it as no more than sibling horseplay. He figured that grown men—as his brothers were—most of whom with wives and children, had better things to do than harbor resentment against their baby brother.

How wrong he was, especially after Joseph shared with them a couple of dreams he had.

"We were binding sheaves of grain in the field when suddenly my sheaf rose and stood upright, while your sheaves gathered around mine and bowed down to it," Joseph told them one day.

If he was expecting warm smiles and a "That is nice, brother," he was woefully wrong.

"Are you out of your mind!" sibling number four Judah railed. "Do you intend to reign over us? Do you really believe you are going to be our ruler?"

Several of the others echoed Judah's sentiments and even spit at Joseph's feet before walking off in a hateful huff. Joseph should have stopped there, but he could not contain himself from sharing with the brothers—and Jacob—his second dream.

"This time," he chirped, "the sun and moon and eleven stars were bowing down to me."

Recognizing himself as "the sun," even Jacob bristled. And the brothers detested him with seething abhorrence. It all came to a head one day as the brothers had gone north to graze Jacob's flocks. Jacob sent Joseph to check on them and make sure they were all right.

Neither he nor Joseph saw what was coming.

From a distance, the brothers caught sight of Joseph. "Here comes that dreamer!" one of them announced. "Let us kill him and be rid of him," they chimed as one—with the notable exception of oldest brother Reuben.

When Joseph reached his siblings, he had barely finished greeting them before they violently grabbed him and led him to a large cistern.

"What is this, my brothers?" a stunned and frightened Joseph pleaded.

"Shut up, dreamer!" they ordered, a smack on the back of the head punctuating the command.

"But brothers…"

Before he could say another word, Joseph found himself at the bottom of the cistern. He cried for mercy, but they simply laughed and walked away. Joseph was too shocked to speak. He heard utterings from above regarding plans to kill him, which was what the brothers would have done had not Reuben objected.

As morning became afternoon, Joseph languished in the cistern. Then he heard a commotion. A band of Ishmaelites was passing through. From below, the horrified youth could hear the brothers bargaining with them. The next thing he knew, he was being hauled from the cistern and sold to the Ishmaelites as a slave.

"Enjoy Egypt, dreamer!" they taunted.

Joseph was too filled with astonishment, dread, and despair to be able to talk; tears were flooding his cheeks. He would never forget the smiling faces of the brothers as the Ishmaelites led him away from the family—and the father—he loved so much. As he was carried off, trembling and sobbing, he could not comprehend his shock to this unfathomable treachery being perpetrated against him. His own brothers had sold him into slavery.

My brothers—they would have killed me had it not been for Reuben. My own brothers…

When he arrived in Egypt as a seventeen-year-old orphan, he was purchased by the head of the household of a powerful Egyptian official, Potiphar, the captain of Pharaoh's guard. However, when Joseph rejected the lustful overtures by Potiphar's wife, he was wrongly accused and incarcerated. A victim of yet another act of treachery.

He would languish in prison for thirteen years.

Then one night, Pharaoh had dreams neither he nor his officials could interpret. Joseph, however, had built a reputation as an expert translator of dreams and was summoned to Pharaoh's presence. At the age of thirty, Joseph's days of imprisonment were over.

God had spoken to him through Pharaoh's dreams. There would be seven years of great abundance in the region, followed by seven devastating years of famine. Joseph had a plan. Pharaoh recognized brilliance when he saw it. He made Joseph his second-in-command and put him in charge of the vast food-storage program that would save his nation.

When the seven years of famine hit, it was bad. People from all over came groveling to Joseph, begging him for food. The grovelers included his brothers. He recognized them—and he shuddered. They had no idea who this Egyptian official was. Joseph turned ashen at the sight of them, the images of twenty years past sweeping over him like a flood.

He would, of course, save their starving families but would not let them off the hook so easily.

He spoke harshly to them. He accused them of being spies. He threw them into prison.

He...just what would he do?

This was what he found himself asking God as he paced his home in the darkness: "Lord, they would have killed me had you not intervened." His voice was shaking.

I could kill them easily, he mused, but then instantly, shamefully, dismissed the monstrous thought.

I could have them beaten. This one struck him as legitimate.

"Why should I not, Lord? Why not at least that?"

But once again, he felt the weight of his evil thoughts.

"Surely, Lord," he prayed, "I cannot simply allow them to get away with what they did to me. Their treachery was unspeakable. Does it not cry out for vengeance?"

He fell to his knees. "Lord, what do I do?"

Then, in the stillness of his troubled soul, he heard the Lord speak. "Joseph, what your brothers did to you, they meant for harm. But I have overruled. I have turned their evil into good. I have brought you here to Egypt to save lives, and that is indeed what you have done and will continue doing. Now, Joseph, love your brothers as I have loved you. Their treachery is for Me to deal with, not you."

It was enough. Joseph would leave them in jail a few more days and throw a scare into them, not for the sake of vengeance, but to bring them to their knees in brokenness and humility. And when they got there, he would reach out to them in love and kindness.

His course set before him, Joseph knew that the next several weeks would be difficult, but a glorious conclusion awaited them.

They despised me, he thought for the final time. *They would have killed me. They sold me into slavery. They committed an abominably treacherous act upon me. But I will love them, Lord, just as you had commanded. I will love them.*

Joseph and You

Imagine Joseph's dilemma.

He was victimized by his brothers in ways nobody should ever have to endure. The treachery inflicted on him was unspeakable. Years later, he was in a position to exact revenge; but instead, he showed loved and compassion. Incredible!

What about you?

What has someone done to you? Have you been victimized in an unforgivable and unfathomable way? Was what was done to you premeditated, heinous, and treacherous? As a Christian, what does God want you to do?

The answer is simple: He wants you to be like Christ.

Check out the words of the apostle Peter: "When they hurled their insults at him [Jesus], he did not retaliate; when he suffered, he made no threats. Instead, he entrusted himself to him who judges justly" (1 Peter 2:23).

Don't retaliate? Don't threaten? Human nature insists that we do! Vengeance must be delved out!

Again, Peter says no! "Do not repay evil with evil or insult with insult, but with blessing, because to this you were called so that you may inherit a blessing" (1 Peter 3:9).

"Okay," you say with a sneer and roll of the eyes, "this is really laying it on thick! Do You know, Lord, what so-and-so did to me?"

He does. And yes, He does understand your anger, hurt, and anguish. He understands it better than you do. But before you dismiss the above verses as naive and unrealistic, take one more look at them, specifically at how they end.

The first verse says, "Instead, he entrusted himself to him who judges justly." And that's the key! No, God is not telling you to ignore the legitimate wrong committed against you; He wants you to deal with it. However, He wants you to do it in His power, not yours. To be a follower of Christ is to take the vicious treachery done against you and give it to God. That's the extent of it. Let God deal with the person who has hurt you. He is more than capable.

The second verse even sweetens the pot a bit. God promises that if you bless the person who has harmed you, then He will bless you in return. Will blessing the person who acted treacherously against you be difficult? Yes, and probably the most difficult thing you will ever have to do in your life. But that's why God promises to bless you; He knows how incredibly difficult it is for you to do.

The world screams for vengeance at every turn. "He did it to me, so I'm going to do it to him!" But God says, "Do nothing to him;

give it to Me. In fact, bless him. And if you do, I will bless you in a wonderful way!"

So, how can you be a Joseph in a wicked, amoral, and treacherous world? Refuse to retaliate, but instead lift your cause to God. Overcome treachery with blessing and hatred with love.

It could well be the greatest triumph of your life!

Moses

Overcoming Shortcomings

"**A**h!" Moses exploded in the barren desert, his sheep disturbed by the sudden outburst. "I cannot speak! I will be laughed out of the Egyptian court!"

Eloquence—or lack of it—was always a problem for this Hebrew who was separated from his family at a young age and—by a miraculous turn—was raised in Egyptian splendor. But those days were over. Moses, now age eighty, had fled Egypt and had spent the past four decades as a humble, unnoticed shepherd in the desert of Midian. Unnoticed, that is, until the God of Israel appeared to him one day while he was tending his flocks.

He was at the foot of Mount Horeb when he noticed a bush being consumed by flames. Well, not really consumed. The fires raged, but the bush was unharmed. "What strange thing is this?" he asked his sheep. "I must have a closer look." As he approached the flames, he suddenly heard a voice pierce the stillness of the wasteland.

"Moses! Moses!"

The shepherd was startled. "Here I am," was all he could manage to say.

"Do not come any closer," the voice said. "Take off your sandals, for the place where you are standing is holy ground."[8]

Trembling, Moses sat, removed his shoes, then assumed a kneeling position.

The voice continued. "I am the God of your father, the God of Abraham, the God of Isaac, and the God of Jacob."

Moses remained frozen, unable to look upon the One who inhabited the flame.

The voice trumpeted on. "I have indeed seen the misery of my people in Egypt, so I have come down to rescue them from the hand of the Egyptians and to bring them into a land flowing with milk and honey. So now, go. I am sending you to Pharaoh to bring my people the Israelites out of Egypt."[9]

The Lord paused, as if giving Moses the opportunity to digest all that had just occurred. His consideration was appreciated as Moses, still trembling at the bush's continuous burning, kept mulling the impossible words he had just heard.

"I am the God…I have seen the misery of my people…I am sending you to Pharaoh…"

Why would the Lord send me? Moses thought, puzzled, and agonizingly so, over the incomprehensible directive. *I can barely put two sentences together without stumbling over my words. Am I to go to the most powerful man on earth and demand that he free my fellow Hebrews?*

It was too much for Moses.

---

[8] Exodus 3:5

[9] Exodus 3:7–8, 10

"But who am I, Lord," he stammered, "that I should go to Pharaoh and bring the Israelites out of Egypt?"

He realized that he had just questioned God's will, but it was certainly not of pride, but rather fear, insecurity, and bewilderment.

God was patient. "I will be with you."

Moses knew that should have been enough, but he was rattled and could not fathom what the God of Israel was asking him to do. "Suppose, Lord," he said cowering, "I go to the Israelites and say to them, 'The God of your fathers has sent me to you,' and they ask me, 'What is his name?' Then what shall I tell them?"

God continued to be patient. "Tell them, I AM WHO I AM. This is what you are to say to the Israelites: 'I AM has sent me to you.'"[10]

Moses felt the enormous weight of the God of the universe and His extraordinary disclosure. He was aware that He had been the first human being to whom God had ever revealed His most divine name.

But the Lord wasn't through. "Moses, tell the people of Israel, 'The Lord, the God of your fathers—the God of Abraham, Isaac, and Jacob—appeared to me and said: I have watched over you and have seen what has been done to you in Egypt. And I have promised to bring you up out of your misery in Egypt into a land flowing with milk and honey.'"[11]

---

[10] Exodus 3:14

[11] Exodus 3:16–17

Moses still could not comprehend it all. *I am to say all this?* he incredulously wondered. "But what if they do not believe me or listen to me and say, 'The Lord did not appear to you'?"

He knew he was pushing the Lord's patience. The Lord indulged him, though, telling Moses to throw his staff on the ground. Moses recoiled in fear as it turned into a snake. He ran from it, hid behind a rock, then returned.

"Moses," God said, "reach out your hand and take it by the tail."

Trembling and perspiring profusely, Moses slowly reached out his hand. The snake turned back into a staff. Moses was overwhelmed, his heart about to crash through the wall of his chest.

And yet God was still not finished. "Moses, put your hand inside your cloak."

Easy enough. He did it. But when he pulled his hand back out, he was devastated to find it turned snowy white. Leprosy. He gazed at his hand in horror and felt like fainting.

"Put your hand back in your cloak," God mercifully ordered.

Moses did, then pulled it out again. His hand was restored. *What kind of all-powerful God is this? And why has He appeared to me?*

God was still not finished. "If the children of Israel do not believe you or pay attention to the first miraculous sign, they may believe the second. But if they do not believe these two signs or listen to you, take some water from the Nile and pour it on the dry ground. The water you take from the river will become blood on the ground."[12]

It should have been enough for Moses, but he still wanted a way out. "Oh, Lord," he desperately objected, "I have never been eloquent, neither in the past nor since you have spoken to your servant. I am slow of speech and tongue."[13]

Moses detected a trace of annoyance in the Lord's voice. "Who gave man his mouth? Who makes him deaf or mute? Who gives him sight or makes him blind? Is it not I, the Lord? Now go; I will help you speak and will teach you what to say."[14]

Again, it should have been enough, but … "Please, Lord," Moses desperately petitioned, falling to his knees "I cannot speak. Send someone else to do it."

There was a frightful pause. "I will send your brother Aaron to speak in your place," God angrily conceded. "He will speak to the people for you, and it will be as if he were your mouth and as if you were God to him. But take this staff in your hand so you can perform miraculous signs with it."

It was the final word, and Moses had no more objections.

"I will be laughed out of the Egyptian court," Moses proclaimed as he returned to his home to tell his wife Zipporah and father-in-law Jethro all that happened. He was self-conscious of his oral

---

[12] Exodus 4:8–9
[13] Exodus 4:10
[14] Exodus 4:11–12

shortcomings, slipping and sliding all over his words as he shared the incident with them.

They must think I am out of my mind! he concluded. *I can hardly tell two people I love this story, let alone speak to a king and lead a nation.* Moses felt the incredible shame of his speech. *Curse my mouth! Why can I not speak eloquently? Why?*

He wanted to ask the Lord if He was sure about all this, but he dare not question the will of the great I AM again. The Lord had made Himself clear and would not relent.

Several weeks later, when Moses and Aaron arrived in Egypt to speak to the elders of Israel, Moses spoke first. "My brothers," he said, "please gather around."

The words flowed smoothly, and though speaking them timidly, they possessed a power that was beyond himself. The people gathered at once. "The God of our fathers has sent me," he said, amazed at the sudden clarity of his speech. "He has promised freedom for our people. Our days of bondage are nearing their end."

He paused and was amazed. He had spoken clearly, and all who were gathered hinged on his every word. He introduced Aaron, and his brother delivered God's words to the people. But Moses did not hear them. He was too stunned to listen. What had just happened? What of his stuttering and lack of eloquence? What of his inability to speak clearly? What of his cowardice? What of his shortcomings?

They had all vanished. God had chosen him and shone His glory upon Him. He had removed from the lowly shepherd that which hindered him from serving the God of Israel. God had allowed him to overcome his wretched shortcomings.

I am now ready to serve you, Lord. I am ready to face whatever You put before me.

Send me now, Lord. Send me now!

Moses and You

God summoned Moses to do a great work. In reply, Moses dictated to the Lord a list of his defects and shortcomings.

God responded, "Who gave man his mouth? Who makes him deaf or mute? Who gives him sight or makes him blind? Is it not I, the Lord? Now go; I will help you speak and will teach you what to say" (Exodus 4:11–12).

And yet Moses *still* argued.

Do you, too, argue with God, or at least question Him for using you for a divine purpose? What do you see when you look in the mirror? Are you short? Do you have unsightly skin? Are you insecure and loathe bringing attention to yourself? Are you by nature a weak person who hates conflict and confrontation? Like Moses, do you have a speech defect? Are you confined to a wheelchair? What are your shortcomings?

Everybody has at least one.

And yet you feel strongly that the Lord is leading you to do something on His behalf. Perhaps you are to tell someone that you are praying for them. Maybe He wants you to share the Gospel with your workmate. It could be that the Lord wants to send you overseas to do missionary work, but you are in a wheelchair.

"Lord," you say, "can't You see my shortcomings? Are You really sure You have the right person? Surely, so-and-so would be a much better choice."

God, however, is not budging.

"Who gives you your mouth?" God replies. "Who gives you confidence despite your insecurity? Who gives you the ability to be mobile despite your wheelchair? Who gives you boldness to proclaim the saving grace of my Son despite your shyness? Isn't it I, my beloved? Isn't it I who scoffs at your shortcomings and gives you wings of eagles on which to soar?"

The message is clear: it is God who equips. You look in the mirror and see shortcomings. God looks at you and sees a vessel through which He will do great things. You consider your life and see failure. God looks at you and says, "Through me, you will bring your workmate to Christ." You look at your scars and say, "I am hideous." God looks at you and says, "You are beautiful in every way."

God told the prophet Samuel, "The Lord does not look at the things man looks at. Man looks at the outward appearance, but the Lord looks at the heart" (1 Samuel 16:7). The heart is exactly what God saw when he looked at Moses. Despite his shortcomings, God saw a man of humility and faith who would carry out His will. And when God sees you, He looks past every shortcoming you have and peers straight into your heart. It is all that matters to Him, and all that counts for His kingdom.

So, if God is telling you to go, then do so in His strength.

He pays no heed to your shortcomings, and neither should you!

Naomi

OVERCOMING TRAGEDY

←«»→

Impoverished. Widowed. Sonless. A decade-long legacy of loss, sorrow, and tragedy.

"Oh, Lord, You have laid a burden on me that is too much for me to bear. Please withdraw Your hand of judgment from me."

It was more of an embittered accusation than a plea for mercy. But now was not the time to rail against God; Naomi had a crucial decision to make. As she paced alongside the main road that led out of the heathen nation of Moab, Naomi rehearsed her words. Two women and three mules were awaiting her decision. Satisfied that she had found the right words, she returned to her companions. "Ruth, Orpah, please come here."

The two young women obeyed. Naomi inhaled deeply and gathered herself.

"As you know, my dear daughters, it was ten years ago when a terrible famine struck my hometown of Bethlehem in Israel, bringing us here." The women already knew the story. "I opposed the move. I told my husband that we were God's people and that we belonged in the land He had given us. But Elimelech was a stubborn man. He said, 'Naomi, if we are God's people, then why has He turned His back on us.'"

The younger women nodded respectfully.

"Elimelech," Naomi continued, "was convinced that God had abandoned us, so when he heard that food was bountiful here in Moab, he moved us here." Her eyes began to well up. "And we know how that decision turned out. Elimelech—may his soul rest in peace—died a few years later, and then my two sons married each of you even though our law forbids marriage of Israelites to Moabites."

Naomi noticed her daughters-in-law's hurt expressions and quickly sought to mend them. "I mean no offense," she said. "You two have been blessings beyond measure to me. And now, with the deaths of Mahlon and Kilion to the plague, I am left bereft of husband and sons, as you are of spouses. And what is worse, all three of us are impoverished. We have nothing."

"It seems," Orpah ventured, "that our grief unites us."

"It does, my dear," Naomi concurred, "but to what end?"

"What do you mean?" Ruth asked suspiciously.

"It means, my daughters, that I must insist that you turn back and return to your homes."

Naomi's bluntness stunned the younger women. "Do not be alarmed at my words," Naomi continued. "What have I to give you if you continue this trip home to Bethlehem with me? I have nothing but our property, and that cannot sustain you. The Lord has stretched out His arm to afflict me, and me only. I have nothing to offer you by way of security. You are both young. Please, return to your fathers' homes and begin life anew."

The two women began to weep. "How can we abandon you at such at time?" Orpah asked.

Naomi assured her. "You are not abandoning me, dear. That you have come this far with me is a wonderful act of kindness. Please, turn back and go home."

Orpah looked at Ruth, who quickly dropped her gaze to the ground. Finding no support there, she turned back to Naomi. "Please, my daughter, I absolutely insist."

Orpah released an anguished wail and embraced Naomi. "Could you ever forgive me if I desert you?"

"There would be nothing to forgive, my dear. And besides, I would consider it wisdom, not desertion."

Orpah had run out of objections. After another show of grief and making her final farewells, she took hold of her mule that carried her possessions and headed back to her father's home.

Naomi turned to Ruth. "You *must* do the same, dearest."

"No, Mother, I cannot."

"But Ruth, the Lord's hand of affliction is heavy upon me. I have nothing for you..."

"No, Mother," Ruth countered, her tone firm, her words insistent. "Don't urge me to leave you or to turn back from you. Where you go I will go, and where you stay I will stay. Your people will be my people and your God my God. Where you die I will die, and there I will be buried. May the Lord deal with me, be it ever so severely, if anything but death separates you and me."[15]

Naomi wanted to argue but could not. Ruth's bold proclamation had staggered her and rendered her dumbfounded. "Very well, then," she stuttered, "let us go to Bethlehem."

Upon their arrival a few days later, they were greeted by a town shocked by Naomi's return. They had heard of all that had befallen her and had no idea how to comfort her. "Welcome home, Naomi," the women said softly.

Naomi stopped and looked at them. "My friends, please do not call me Naomi any longer. The name 'Pleasant' no longer applies to me. Instead, call me Mara, for the Almighty Himself has made my life bitter. He has afflicted me and brought misfortune upon me."

After a week, Naomi's wretchedness knew no bounds. She still felt the relentless pangs of her tragic fate and the dreary emptiness of her husbandless and sonless house. Ruth, on the other hand, knew there were dire needs that must be met. Nourishment being one of them.

"We are running out of food, Mother," she said. "Let me go to the fields and pick up the leftover grain behind anyone in whose eyes I find favor."

Naomi had no choice but to consent as Ruth set out for the nearby fields.

---

[15] Ruth 1:16–17

Alone in the house for the first time since her return, Naomi's misery was never more acute. She felt the horrible loneliness of her existence, the terrible bitterness of her soul. "Oh, Lord," she cried falling to her knees, "why have You afflicted me so? Why have You forsaken me as You have?"

She wallowed in her misery all day until Ruth suddenly came rushing through the door. "Mother, please, come outside and see."

Naomi was baffled. Following Ruth, she found on the ground before her house a week's supply of barley. "Where did you get this?" she asked stunned as she gazed over the impressive haul.

"I harvested in the field of a man named Boaz. He showed remarkable kindness and mercy to me."

Naomi considered the name. "Yes, I know Boaz," she said, detecting an unexpected twinge of hope. "He is a very close relative of ours and a wonderful man. Yes, Ruth, glean only in his fields. He will look out for you."

Over the next few months, Boaz continued to do exactly what Naomi said he would do, and the two women had no lack of provision. But Naomi was not satisfied. One morning, before Ruth left for the field, Naomi stopped her. "I must speak with you, my dear."

"Yes, Mother."

"I can no longer sleep. My mind is consumed with thoughts of you."

"Then, please, speak what you must."

"My daughter, should I not try to find a home for you, where you will be well provided for?" Ruth listened quietly. "I want you to do something," Naomi continued. "Tonight, Boaz will be winnowing barley on the threshing floor. I want you to wash and perfume yourself and put on your best clothes. Go down to the threshing floor, and when he lies down, go and uncover his feet and lie down. He will tell you what to do."[16]

"You want me to offer myself to him in marriage?"

"Yes, my love. I know he is quite a bit older than you, but he will provide for you for the rest of your life. You will be a woman of means and security. Will you do this, my love?"

"I will do whatever you say, Mother."

Naomi watched as Ruth left for the fields. When she was out of sight, Naomi kneeled. "Lord," she said softly, "I am tired of fighting with You and inflicting my hostility upon You. If You would but make this marriage a reality, then I will die contently. Oh, Lord, I know I do not deserve Your mercy, but if You do this one thing, then You will have my gratitude for eternity."

One year later, Naomi sat as the guest of honor of the women of Bethlehem. On her lap was her two-day-old grandson, Obed.

"Praise be to the Lord, who has given you a son!" the women exuded. "He will renew your life and sustain you in your old age. For your daughter-in-law, who loves you and who is better to you than seven sons, has given him birth."

---

[16] Ruth 3:3–4

Ruth came up behind Naomi and embraced her. Naomi wanted to return the loving gesture, but her hands were already filled. Then, suddenly, all seemed to go silent. In that moment of inexpressible joy, Naomi felt the presence of God as never before.

Dearest Lord, she gloried in the inner recesses of her soul, *you have turned my misery into joy; my tragedy into triumph. My heart is yours. My soul is yours. I am yours. Always.*

Naomi and You

Naomi's burden was indeed heavy. Within a ten-year period, she had lost her husband and two sons. It was a tragic series of events that mortified her.

What about you?

Have you suffered great tragedy? Have you lost a loved one? Parent? Child? Spouse? Dear friend? If so, you understand what Naomi went through. If you have endured such tragedy, then you know that the pain never really goes away. However, through the Lord, the pain can be diminished over the years as you allow His comfort to inhabit you.

King David was certainly someone who knew tragedy, having outlived several sons and his beloved best friend, as well as bore the rape of his beautiful daughter. David cried out often to the Lord and knew that He was always there for him. "May your unfailing love be my comfort, according to your promise to your servant" (Psalm 119:76).

For David, the source of God's comfort was His "unfailing love." This also should be a great source of comfort for you. No matter how deep your pain, how overwhelming your suffering, you can be assured that God loves you with a love that can never fail. He mourns with you and understands the extent of the tragic events you are facing.

In tragedy, turn to God; He will *not* fail.

God exhibits his unfailing love to you by way of divine comfort. The apostle Paul writes, "Praise be to the God and Father of our Lord Jesus Christ, the Father of compassion and the God of all comfort, who comforts us in all our troubles" (2 Corinthians 1:3–4). Notice the word *all*. What have you experienced? Is it too small for God's attention? Of course not. Is it too large for Him to handle? Certainly not. Even if the entire world turns its back on you, God never will. He is there to comfort you in your time of distress and trouble—all of it!

Another way to cope with tragedy is to bring relief to others who have experienced it. Notice how Naomi, despite her severe anguish, looked out for Ruth's welfare by determining to see her well married.

Our 2 Corinthians passage echoes this truth: "Praise be to the God and Father of our Lord Jesus Christ, the Father of compassion and the God of all comfort, who comforts us in all our troubles, *so that we can comfort those in any trouble with the comfort we ourselves receive from God*" (2 Corinthians 1:3–4, italic added).

Notice how, after you begin to regain your strength, God not only encourages, but also *expects* you to take the comfort He gave you and share it with someone else who is suffering. Comforting others is a wonderful way to help relieve your own pain.

Tragedy in this life is constant and unavoidable. But as a Christian, you will never experience it *without* God's unfailing love accompanying it. Cling to His love and comfort and you will ultimately overcome the tragedy that has befallen you!

Hannah

OVERCOMING MISERY

→«»→

Each year, Hannah felt her misery ever more profoundly. Much of this had to do with the pace at which Peninnah bore children for their husband Elkanah. It was bad enough that the Lord had allowed the younger woman to be fruitful. And it was worse when Peninnah persecuted Hannah because of it. It surely added an anguish that weighed heavily on Hannah's soul.

"Oh, Lord," Hannah prayed, "please lift your judgment from me and open my womb. My plight is worse than I can bear."

When Hannah first married Elkanah, she was happy. After all, her goodhearted and doting husband loved her and was wholly devoted to her. Elkanah was demonstrative in his affection for his wife, and for this, Hannah was grateful. But after five years of marriage, when it was apparent that the Lord had closed Hannah's womb, Elkanah, knowing the importance of children to help work the fields and carry on his name, married a local woman who would give him children. Peninnah was not as attractive or gracious as Hannah, but she was younger—and fertile.

Over the next seven years, she produced for Elkanah a bevy of sons and daughters that had justified—to his way of thinking—the taking of a second wife.

Hannah, however, was not as easily convinced. Whenever the family traveled to the tabernacle at Shiloh to worship and offer sacrifices to the Lord, Elkanah gave single portions of meat to Peninnah and her children. But to his beloved Hannah, with whom he was hopelessly in love and pitied for her barrenness, he gave a double portion.

And Peninnah fumed! "Well, well," she mocked Hannah as she toted her offering to the place of sacrifice. Her voice sent shivers through Hannah. "I see that our ever-benevolent husband has yet again abundantly supplied you."

Hannah restrained her anger. "Please, Peninnah, this is a wonderful time for not only our people, but also our family. We are here today to give glory to God and to worship him. Can you not lay aside your hostility for today?"

"Dear Hannah," she goaded, "I am not hostile. Why would you think of such a thing? I was only noting how generous Elkanah was in giving you such a large portion."

"Yes," Hannah replied uneasily, "he has been generous."

"I mean, if that is what he believes it is going to take to...oh, never mind."

That was good enough for Hannah. "Very well, then, Peninnah. I will go and offer my sacrifice and..."

"Of course," Peninnah added, unable to contain herself, "it never does any good, you know."

Hannah struggled to hold her tongue as Peninnah fiercely pressed on. "For years, he has been giving you a double portion of meat, and it has accomplished nothing. I, on the other hand, receive but a miniscule single portion, and within the year, I always deliver to Elkanah a new child. I wonder why this is. Do you ever wonder about this, Hannah?"

She did and though it conflicted with her every instinct, Hannah chose tact. "The Lord has been good to you, Peninnah. He has given you a wonderfully fruitful womb and strong, healthy children. You are indeed a blessed woman."

"Blessed!" Peninnah exploded. "You called me blessed?"

Hannah tried to calm her. "Of course, Peninnah. You are the mother of many children and…"

"And what, Hannah? What do I have besides that?"

"Is this not enough?"

"*You* would think this is, Hannah, would you not?"

"What do you mean, Peninnah?"

"How can we live together day after day, and yet you can still ask me this? Are you so selfish, Hannah, that you cannot see the torment I must persistently endure?"

Hannah bit her lip.

"It is our husband, Hannah," Peninnah continued to rage. "He is the cause of my great suffering!"

"What great suffering, Peninnah?"

"Of course, *you* would not notice, Hannah. He loves you!"

"But he loves you, too, Peninnah."

"Please, Hannah, you are blind. I can see how he looks at you. Even on his worst days, when he comes home exhausted from the fields because they have produced nothing, he takes one look at you and his entire world lights up. You are the sun and the moon and the stars to him!"

"Really, Peninnah..."

"But what about me!" Peninnah railed on, ignoring Hannah's attempt to steady her. "How does he look at me?" She then pointed. "I am no more than one of those slabs of meat to him! He only requires me to produce children. If he had his way, he would keep you and the children and banish me."

"This is silly, Peninnah..."

"Silly! How can you say such a thing? How can you be so cruel and unfeeling, Hannah?"

"But Peninnah..."

"I have heard enough, Hannah! Go make your sacrifice, as if it will do any good."

Hannah turned to leave, but Peninnah stopped her. "You know, Hannah," she said venomously, "if Elkanah gave *me* and *all* my children double portions of meat, we would be impoverished. All those children...just think of it, Hannah... all those children. All of *my* children."

Hannah *did* think of it, and it tore at her. The thorns of its savage reality pricked and stabbed her emotions, leaving them frayed, bloodied, and exposed. The meat suddenly felt very heavy as she lugged it to Hophni and Phinehas, the two sons of the high priest, Eli. She watched them set the portions aflame, their smoke curling up to the heavens. Hannah wondered if her prayers ascended the same way, and if the Lord even heard them.

Still deeply troubled, Hannah made her way to the outer court of the tabernacle. She greeted Eli, who sat by the door, then found a private corner where she could pray. She had never felt such bitterness and misery in her life and could barely speak. She began to pray, but the words would not come out; she was too overwrought. Besides, she thought, she had been praying for years for children, but the Lord had not delivered.

Suddenly, she had a stunning revelation, as if the Lord were directing her. Though too overcome to speak, she felt the words forming, breathing, and taking on a life of their own.

"O Lord Almighty, if you will only look upon your servant's misery and remember me, and not forget your servant but give her a son," she petitioned, her lips moving, but no sound accompanying them, "then I will give him to you for all the days of his life, and no razor will ever be used on his head."

She had said it. If the Lord would at last open her womb and give her a son, then she would give the boy back to Him at the time of his weaning. She also vowed that her child would be set apart to serve the Lord for the rest of his life. It was an incredible—if not daring— vow, but Hannah felt peace the instant she uttered the words.

A few days later, Hannah and Elkanah lay together, and shortly after, the Lord opened Hannah's womb. She felt the glory and wonder of it, her misery and anguish vanishing as her empty belly suddenly awoke with the miracle of new life.

Elkanah rejoiced with his grateful wife, and the entire village celebrated—with the notable exception of Peninnah.

When the child was born, Hannah named him "Samuel"—which means, "God hears"—saying, "because I asked the Lord for him."

Every day with little Samuel was euphoric, each to be cherished as if it were her last with him. And, in some ways, each day was. How three years passed so quickly, Hannah had no idea, but at last Samuel was weaned and it was time to deliver the child she had awaited for so long to the tabernacle in Shiloh to begin his service to the Lord. Turning him over to Eli was the most difficult thing she ever had to do, but with the Lord's strength, she did so with great peace.

Living a short distance away, Hannah would visit Samuel yearly, assuring that the boy would know who his mother was. Hannah would have a profound influence on Samuel as he grew to become a prophet and leader of Israel.

The Lord, too, was merciful to Hannah, blessing her and Elkanah with three sons and two daughters.

As the years passed and Samuel grew, Hannah rejoiced—her trips to Shiloh transformed from misery to jubilation and exaltation. God had delivered her in a mighty way, erasing the devastation of her soul and lifting her to heights of exhilaration she could never have imagined. Where once her mouth was incapable of prayer, now it could no longer be silenced.

"My heart rejoices in the Lord," she extoled. "In the Lord, my horn is lifted high. My mouth boasts over my enemies, for I delight in your deliverance. There is no one holy like the Lord; there is no one besides you; there is no Rock like our God."[17]

The misery that had for so long enslaved her had become but a distant memory.

Hannah and You

Hannah was intimately acquainted with misery as her long years of barrenness and Peninnah's persecution tormented her soul.

After she prayed to God, she was comforted by the high priest Eli, who told her, "Go in peace, and may the God of Israel grant you what you have asked of him" (1 Samuel 1:17). Hannah then, "went her way and ate something, and her face was no longer downcast" (v. 18).

Notice how Hannah suddenly felt the Lord's comfort *before* she became pregnant. Why? The Lord gave her peace. Again, read how the Lord did not yet tell Hannah that she would have a child, and yet "her face was no longer downcast."

Perhaps, like Hannah, you know what true misery is. You may have experienced a terrible event or loss in your life, and your entire soul is overcome by sorrow and depression. Each day is a struggle to

---

[17] 1 Samuel 2:1–2

get out of bed because you know that nothing but gloom and distress await you.

However, if you know Jesus Christ as your Lord and Savior, then you have a reason to smile. Despite the anguish of your heart, God gives you several reasons to rejoice.

First, understand that God knows what you are going through. Psalm 139:1–4 assures you that: "O Lord, you have searched me and you know me. You know when I sit and when I rise; you perceive my thoughts from afar. You discern my going out and my lying down; you are familiar with all my ways. Before a word is on my tongue you know it completely, O Lord." This is intimacy of the most precious kind. God knows you better than you know yourself, and He is aware of *everything* you are feeling and experiencing. You do not carry your burden alone!

Second, in your misery, God is near. The apostle Paul writes, "For just as the sufferings of Christ flow over into our lives, so also through Christ our comfort overflows" (2 Corinthians 1:5). In context, Paul is referring to the suffering of Christian persecution, and though your suffering likely derives from a different source, it is still real and deeply felt. God feels it, too! This verse assures you that being "in Christ" (Romans 8:1) is beneficial, one way of which is God's pouring of comfort into you in times of desperate misery and melancholy.

Third, the prophet Isaiah also sounds a resounding chord regarding God's great comfort: "Shout for joy, O heavens; rejoice, O earth; burst into song, O mountains! For the Lord comforts his people and will have compassion on his afflicted ones" (Isaiah 49:13). Are you afflicted on either the outside or inside? Are you in torment? If so, the Lord showers you with His comfort and compassion.

If misery has entered your life, don't despair; things will not always be this way. Reread the above verses and take consolation in the fact that God loves you too much to let you wallow in your despair.

God will banish your misery; you will smile again!

Abigail

Overcoming Marital Distress

←«»→

Abigail was the finest and most gracious of women. Nabal was the most foolish and obscene of men. And yet they were wed to each other.

For Abigail, her twelve-year marriage was a torturous endeavor, one filled with verbal abuse, hostility, and endless distress. Nabal—a drunkard, a wicked disgrace of a husband—made life miserable for his devoted wife. Yet Abigail endured it with grace.

However, what challenged her most was the loneliness and lovelessness of her predicament. Despite her husband's numerous faults, Abigail could tolerate it all if he would only love her. If she could but feel his warm embrace or be the grateful recipient of a tender kiss on the cheek every so often, that would be wonderful.

But for Abigail, there would be no love because Nabal was incapable of it. This is the way it always was, and the way it always would be.

For now, however, Abigail's marital sorrows were secondary in light of recent developments.

"Now slow down, Malchus," Abigail gently appealed to Nabal's chief servant, "and start again."

"Yes, madam, of course." Malchus took a deep breath. "As I was saying, all the time our shepherds were in the fields in Carmel, David's men, about six hundred, protected us. In fact, night and day they were a wall around us all the time we were herding our sheep near them."

"I am sure," Abigail concluded, "they were seeking a reward from your master."

"They were. Early this morning, David sent ten men to Master Nabal—I accompanied them myself and heard everything that transpired."

"Tell me what was said, Malchus."

"Speaking for David, one of the messengers said to my master, 'I hear that it is sheep-shearing time. When your shepherds were with us, we did not mistreat them, and the whole time they were at Carmel nothing of theirs was missing. Therefore be favorable toward my young men, since we come at a festive time. Please give your servants and your son David whatever you can find for them.'"[18]

"A proper request, but I fear one not received well by my husband," Abigail surmised.

"You are correct, madam. Master Nabal told them, 'Who is this David? Who is this son of Jesse? Many servants are breaking away from their masters these days. Why should I take my bread and

---

[18] 1 Samuel 25:7–8

water, and the meat I have slaughtered for my shearers, and give it to men coming from who knows where?"[19]

Abigail turned away. "Oh, Lord, help us." She turned back to Malchus. "What happened next?"

"Within an hour, David had formed a contingent of four hundred men armed with swords and spears at their sides. They are heading our way. I believe they intend to destroy our entire household."

Abigail turned pale and began to pace. "Please give me wisdom, Lord," she prayed. "Please give me wisdom."

She regained her composure. "This is what you are to do, Malchus. Gather all the donkeys and collect two hundred loaves of bread, two hundred cakes of pressed figs, two skins of wine, five dressed sheep, a bushel of roasted grain, and one hundred cakes of raisins, and load them on the donkeys. Go to David and pray that we are not too late. I will be riding behind you."

Abigail summoned another servant and had him saddle her donkey to take her to David. As she rode through the hill country of Carmel, she was oblivious to its striking pastoral beauty. Her mind was riled by thoughts of impending doom and utter abhorrence for her reckless husband whose fatal foolishness had brought every male living in his home to the brink of death.

"Oh, Lord, how can I endure such a man?"

She had asked this question on the day her parents informed her that they had arranged her marriage to him for a sizable dowry.

---

[19] 1 Samuel 18:10–11

Abigail, then a beautiful seventeen-year-old with wisdom and discernment far beyond her years, was mortified. She had known much about this man Nabal, the wealthiest man for miles around but also the most wicked and foolish. When in the marketplace, she would notice this lecher who was more than twice her age leering at her. And she would cringe. She stayed as far away from him as possible.

And then she received the unfathomable news from her parents that they had agreed to Nabal's terms of marriage to their daughter. When informed of her parents' decision, Abigail reacted with dignity in their presence, but once alone in her room, she broke down in tears.

"Oh, Lord, how can I endure such a man?"

She would repeat this cry many times over the next twelve years, and every time the Lord's answer came back to her, it would be, *"By My grace."*

The Lord's gentle comfort was enough. It would help carry her through the long years of loneliness and lovelessness. It would carry her through the unbearable curses Nabal would spew at her during drunken rages. It would fortify her through the vindictive threats of divorce whenever she displeased him—with the solemn promise that he would make her a destitute woman. The Lord's grace would bolster her through the vile, bitter hatred and disdain with which Nabal treated everyone in his path. This was life with Nabal, and without the Lord to carry her, Abigail would have crumbled.

Abigail's musings occupied her until she came to a deep, narrow gorge where David was leading his men. Nabal's servants stopped and trembled as David drew his sword.

Abigail quickly dismounted her donkey, ran to David, and fell at his feet. "Please, my Lord," she said, her eyes never leaving the ground, "do not do what you have in mind. Instead, let your wrath fall on me. My husband is a fool—as his name indicates."

She awaited a reaction. "Continue," David said patiently.

"You are the great general of Israel and will one day be our king, but if you take revenge and kill innocent men, you will always carry the guilt of it. Oh, my lord, may no guilt ever beset your reign." She drew a breath and continued. "And now, my lord, please accept these humble gifts that my servants have brought to you. They are richly deserved for all your kindness."

Abigail held her breath.

"Please stand, good woman," David said softly.

At once, Abigail felt a surge of relief. She rose but kept her eyes down.

"Please look at me," David implored.

When she did, Abigail was struck by the warmth of his countenance.

"Praise be to the Lord, who has sent you to me this day," David said warmly. "May you be blessed for your good judgment and for keeping me from bloodshed this day and from avenging myself with my own hands. You are indeed an angel sent from God."

Abigail felt her heart breaking with every word David spoke. She had never been spoken to so gently, and it was wonderful.

David's men gratefully accepted Abigail's gifts.

"Go home in peace," David told Abigail, his hand on her shoulder. "You have saved your husband's household."

Oh, Lord, Abigail prayed as she rode back to her loveless existence, *what kind of man is this? Strength yet tenderness. Power yet compassion. Forcefulness yet respect. Oh, Lord…*

She dreaded walking through the door of her house. When she did, she intended to tell Nabal about all that had happened, but he was hopelessly drunk. She waited until the next day, when he would be sober.

"What is it you want, wife?" Nabal testily asked when he saw her approaching him.

"An incident occurred yesterday that you must know about."

"Fine, just be quick about it."

It took Abigail but three minutes to tell her story, and when she had finished, Nabal inexplicably collapsed, his heart barely beating. Abigail summoned two servants who carried her comatose spouse to his bed. Ten days later, Nabal died.

"Surely, this is your doing, Lord," Abigail surmised.

Following her week of customary mourning, Abigail awoke on the eighth day and wondered what would become of her. She and Nabal had no children, and the property would transfer to Nabal's relatives. She would be cast off. And just as that terrifying reality dawned on her, Malchus came to see her.

"Madam, two messengers from David are here to see you."

At the mere mention of David's name, Abigail felt her spirit begin to soar.

The messenger spoke briefly. "David has sent us to you to take you to become his wife."[20]

Abigail humbly accepted the offer, sent the messengers on their way, and found herself a solitary place. She fell prone to the ground. "Oh, Lord, am I truly to become the wife of a man who will love me? I know nothing of such goodness. Oh, Lord, make me a worthy wife to this man. I have lived in heartache for so long. I know little else."

As she rose, Abigail wiped her tears and summoned her five attendants. By that evening, she would be in David's camp, ready to begin a new life. It would be a life filled with love and affection, tenderness and compassion.

The long, insufferable years of her bitter distress were to become but a mere memory.

Abigail and You

Abigail was in a loveless and bitter marriage.

During the time in which she lived, divorce was not an option for a woman. Therefore, Abigail, described as "intelligent and beautiful" (1 Samuel 25:3), graciously endured the distress of her marriage and waited patiently for the Lord to deliver her.

What about you?

---

[20] 1 Samuel 25:40

Are you trapped in a loveless marriage? As a woman of God, you are hesitant to seek a divorce, though the Bible reluctantly allows it in limited situations (Matthew 5:32, 19:9). You are aware of God's own words: "'I hate divorce,' says the Lord God of Israel" (Malachi 2:16). Therefore, you dutifully and faithfully remain in your marriage, yet all along you are miserable and full of distress.

What's the answer?

The answer is to throw yourself on God's mercy and ask Him for the strength to persevere. When you do, the Lord makes you this promise: "For I am the Lord, your God, who takes hold of your right hand and says to you, 'Do not fear; I will help you'" (Isaiah 41:13). As you bear up under your difficult circumstances, don't be afraid to cry. Don't be reluctant to sprawl yourself on the ground and pour your tears out to God. In return, He will gently and lovingly take hold of your hand and say, "Do not fear; I will help you."

It is a tremendous comfort to know that not only is God aware of your loveless and distressful marriage, but He also longs for you to tell Him about it. The apostle Peter urges you to: "Cast all your anxiety on [God] because he cares for you" (1 Peter 5:7). Note the Lord's wonderful invitation. He *wants* you to lay your burdens upon Him. He encourages you to do so. Why? Because He cares for you. It is as if God is saying, "I know, dear one, that you are trapped in a loveless marriage. I also know that you are trying your best to honor Me despite your pain. I give you My word that I am with you every step of the way."

And even in your worst, most despairing moments, God is there even when you feel that He doesn't even know that you are alive. Yet He is as close as ever. He says, "So do not fear, for I am with you; do not be dismayed, for I am your God. I will strengthen you and help you; I will uphold you with my righteous right hand" (Isaiah 41:10).

Notice in all these passages how God does not necessarily promise to deliver you out of your circumstances; instead, He promises to walk beside you and give you the strength to endure under them.

Do you seek love and affection? Of course you do. But even if your spouse will never be the one to provide them to you, the Lord will *always* supply you with the love you need and deserve.

And He has an abundant supply of love and affection that will never run out!

Bathsheba

OVERCOMING BLATANT SIN

◄—❝❞—►

Bathsheba knew it was time to put Solomon down so he could sleep more comfortably, but she could not bring herself to let go of him.

"Oh, Lord," she quietly prayed, "I still cannot believe you have given him to me. Even after two weeks, I still cannot believe it."

She kissed the infant softly, lowered him toward his bed, hesitated, kissed him again, and then finally forced herself to lay the child down. As she watched him sleep, Bathsheba continued to marvel. "My sin, Lord, was so grievous and blatant, and yet..." She caressed the child's tiny body. "I am so undeserving, Lord. So undeserving."

She was. The daughter of Eliam, among Israel's finest soldiers and one of King David's elite fighting forces of thirty-seven warriors, Bathsheba was raised in affluence. When she reached her upper teen years, Eliam knew it was time to find a husband for her.

He did not have to go far to look. One of the younger of David's elite fighters was a man named Uriah, whose faithfulness to the king and courage on the battlefield caught Eliam's attention. Eliam identified Uriah as a worthy husband for Bathsheba, and when his daughter was old enough to marry, Eliam made the arrangements.

Bathsheba was certainly not displeased. Uriah was tall, strong, handsome, brave, considerate, and loyal. He was devoted to Bathsheba and thrilled to be married to her.

She felt the same way about Uriah. At first. Though she appreciated his devotion to her, Bathsheba was not nearly as enamored with Uriah's devotion to David. Yes, Uriah was a loyal husband, but he was far more a loyal soldier who would sacrifice his life for his king *before* he would lay it down for his wife. Uriah's loyalty to David kept him away from home often, whether for a few extra hours of training or fighting on the frontlines of battle.

After five years, Bathsheba was sad. She knew that Uriah would never stop loving her, but the problem was that he was hardly ever around to show it. She longed for him to one day come home early from a day of training, take her hand, and vow to dedicate more time to building their love and marriage. However, she knew it would never happen as Uriah was hopelessly faithful to the king and always would be.

Bathsheba had become lonely, neglected, angry, and shunned. She felt abandoned. She longed for love and attention. She longed for someone to tell her how beautiful and desirable she was. It had been a long time. Then one evening, when Uriah was on the battlefield and as the sun was setting, she decided to bathe on her porch. She and Uriah lived in one of the tangle of houses and courtyards nestled in the shadow of David's palace, at which she often looked up and saw the king as he entertained guests, always wishing she could be one of them.

As her attendants assisted her, Bathsheba's mind was occupied, and she lingered at her bathing much longer than necessary. Her maids noted that her dalliance made her a visual target for those living in homes situated higher up the hill and that perhaps it would be wise to go inside.

She agreed and went into the house. However, as she dressed in her nightclothes, she heard a knock on the door. "Odd that someone should be visiting at this time," she said, talking to herself having become a habit long ago.

She waited in the main living quarters of her house to find out who was at the door. "Madam," one of her attendants said while entering, "a messenger from King David is in the entryway."

At the mention of the king's name, Bathsheba began to feel a surge of excitement swirl through her. She rose quickly. "What does he want?"

"He said that the king has invited you to join him for a late dinner."

Bathsheba was astonished. She did not even know that David knew she existed. "Is he not at war with his troops?"

"I only know what the messenger told me, madam."

Bathsheba could hardly contain herself. "Please inform the messenger that I need twenty minutes to make myself presentable, and then I will accompany him to the palace."

As Bathsheba hurriedly fixed her hair and applied a generous amount of perfume and cosmetics, she felt as giddy as the day she met Uriah. *What a strange turn of events,* she mused. *What will I say to the king? Which wife will accompany him as he greets me? Perhaps Abigail. I have heard so many good things about her.*

Her musings would soon be answered as she made her way to the palace and was ushered into the king's presence. David—who was alone—smiled and approached her. "Daughter of Eliam," he said, taking her hand, "I welcome you to my palace. You are welcome."

The king's touch ignited Bathsheba with shivers of exhilaration. From the instant she met his eyes, she knew exactly what would happen that night.

As she returned home before dawn the following morning, she was still filled with elation. The king had fulfilled her every desire.

A few days later, Bathsheba realized that she was pregnant and sent word to David. "I will handle this, Bathsheba," was the reply.

A week later, Uriah was dead. A week after that—Bathsheba's time of mourning was over by then—David asked her to become his wife. And she was wretchedly miserable.

What had happened? she wondered as cold, harsh reality cascaded over her in waves.

She had an adulterous night with the king and became pregnant. Uriah had conveniently died on the battlefield, the unholy maneuverings of David. And she was now married to him.

What had happened?

"What have I done, Lord? What have I done? Poor, poor Uriah. My husband. Oh, Uriah. What have I done?"

She was consumed by guilt and longed for the birth of her and David's baby. "New life, new hope," she tried to convince herself.

But as the baby was being delivered, Bathsheba looked at the midwife and knew that something was wrong. "The boy has a terrible fever," she told Bathsheba.

One week later, he was dead. And Bathsheba was shattered. "Surely, Lord, this is punishment for my blatant sin. You are just, Lord, but why did You take this child's life and not mine?"

Her soul was in misery, as was David's, who spent several days comforting her. "What have we done, David? What have we done?"

"Our sin is great indeed, Bathsheba. The fault is mine. I have brought this ruin upon us."

"Now what, my husband? What do we do now?"

"We throw ourselves upon the Lord's mercy. It is abundant."

"But, my husband, how abundant? Uriah…oh, David, what have we done to Uriah? And our child…"

"We must pray, Bathsheba. We must pray."

And pray she did. Bathsheba kept herself secluded, spending hours in prayer and refusing to eat at the king's table. She felt unworthy to do so. "Oh, Lord," she cried out in her anguish, "what right do I have to even be alive when Uriah and my son have perished? What have I done, Lord? What have I done?"

That night, for the first time since the child's death, Bathsheba and David lay together. A few days later, Bathsheba was pregnant.

And she trembled. "Oh, Lord, no, not again. I cannot endure it. I cannot lose another child. Oh, Lord, if you must take a life for my horrible sin, then take mine and spare this child."

The next nine months were grueling for Bathsheba, who prayed daily for the life of the child, fearing that he would encounter the same fate as his brother.

As Bathsheba delivered the child, she terrifyingly looked at the midwife. The woman was smiling broadly. "He is perfect, madam," she said.

David and Bathsheba called him Solomon.

Two days later, as Bathsheba held the blessed child, David came to see her. "I have just spoken to the prophet Nathan," he said, a tear trickling down his cheek. "He gave me this message from God: 'You may continue to call your child Solomon, but I have also given him a name, Jedidiah.' Tell me, Bathsheba, is this not a wonderful name? Is our Lord not a wonderful and merciful God?"

Bathsheba thought for a second. *Jedidiah. "Loved by the Lord."*

She smiled. "Yes, my husband, He *is* wonderful and merciful. Far more than I ever could have dreamed."

And now, two weeks later, as Bathsheba sat watching tiny Solomon—Jedidiah—sleep, she could not contain herself. She rose quickly and left the room. "I am overwhelmed, Lord. Why have you bestowed this goodness upon such a vile and blatant sinner as myself? I am so unworthy, Lord. So unworthy."

She wiped her tears and composed herself. "I know, Lord, that I will never understand this unfathomable grace of Yours, but I humbly accept it. I know I can never repay You, but may I ever walk before You in righteousness. Oh, Lord, You are too wonderful for me to comprehend. Too wonderful!"

Bathsheba and You

David and Bathsheba sinned blatantly—and paid a heavy price for it.

What about you?

Have you sinned blatantly? An affair with a married person? A same-sex relationship? A theft or some form of cheating, such as lying on your taxes? Have you made life miserable for another person? What have you done?

An even more important question is: Can God forgive you? And if so, what do you need to do?

First: Yes, God can—and will with your sincere repentance—forgive you. In fact, he *wants* to do just that! "Who is a God like you, who pardons sin and forgives the transgression of the remnant of his inheritance? You do not stay angry forever but delight to show mercy" (Micah 7:18). As a believer in Jesus Christ, you are part of God's remnant (Romans 11:1–24). As such, you are one to whom God "delights" to show mercy. It is as if God is saying to you, "I know that you have sinned blatantly against Me, but I will not hold your sin against you forever. Come to me *now* and seek forgiveness. I am ready to give it to you!" What a blessed promise!

Second, you must take the initiative and turn to God. Regarding this, the key verse for you to know (and memorize) is 1 John 1:9: "If we confess our sins, he is faithful and just and *will* forgive us our sins and purify us from all unrighteousness" (italic added). The primary Greek word for "confess" is *homologeo*, which basically means "to say the same thing" and then "agree, admit, acknowledge."[21] The important thing is not just expressing the words of confession for what you have done, but admitting and acknowledging that it was indeed a sin. God calls for such honesty not as a way to punish you, but to make you see the wrong of what you have done so as not to repeat it.

True confession (admitting sin) and repentance (turning from it) opens the door to God's forgiveness and restoration. However, please remember that God never promises to *always* take away the earthly consequences of your sin, though He may choose to do so. After all, David repented in tears and anguish, yet the Lord still allowed his first child with Bathsheba to die.

However, what He *does* promise is to bury your sin and erase it from His memory. Isaiah 1:18 says, "Though your sins are like scarlet, they shall be as white as snow; though they are red as crimson, they shall be like wool." God's desire is forgiveness *and* restoration. He wants to use you for His kingdom and can only do so fully if sin is dealt with and purged. Despite your sin, God encourages you to forget what is behind and strain toward what is ahead (Philippians 3:13).

---

[21] http://bible.org/question/what-are-greek-and-hebrew-words-%E2%80%9Cconfess%E2%80%9D

So, have you sinned blatantly? Do you truly seek God's forgiveness? He gave Bathsheba a son who would become king of Israel. He will do amazing things for you, too.

You only need to ask Him. He is waiting!

Widow of Zarephath
OVERCOMING POVERTY

←«»→

Baal had failed miserably. He was a fraud.

As Saida[22] watched her emaciated son lay on his bed fighting to stay alive, she knew that her misplaced faith in the fertility non-god of the Sidonians was in vain. She was in the throes of poverty—physically, emotionally, and spiritually. Life had been cruel to her the past two years since her husband died. Trying to eke out an existence for her boy, now ten, and herself was the all-encompassing objective of her life. She would often go to bed wondering if there would be any food for them the next day.

It had gotten *that* bad. And it got even worse when the drought hit. A prophet in Israel predicted it, and it had happened. It had spread its tentacle-like fury throughout the land of the Hebrews and into her nation of Lebanon. Her village of Zarephath was particularly hit hard.

Perhaps this dire prediction should have been enough for her to place her trust in this God whose will could so easily outweigh

---

[22] Character not named in the Bible. Name added to enrich story.

that of her own nation's deity. But seeing her son's protruding ribs through his thin tunic did nothing to lead her to *want* to have faith in anything.

The first year following her husband's premature death was bearable. He had left them with their humble home and a couple of olive trees. A small nearby barley field also proved convenient. But then came the drought, and with it the eventual death of the olive trees and drying of the barley field. The generosity of once-sympathetic neighbors also evaporated, and Saida and her son were destitute.

She knew that there was nowhere else to turn. The deathly poverty that settled over the land was about to claim two more victims, and she resigned herself to the fact that she and her son were spending their final day on earth before heading into a deep and dark unknown eternity.

As her boy lay sleeping—and dying—she made one final survey of all the food she had left: a mere handful of flour and a fistful of olive oil. She looked at them and decided that if she and her boy were going to die, then they do so using the last of their resources.

Wanting to cook one final meal for them, Saida went out to the lifeless field next to her house to gather some sticks. The scorching sun shone mercilessly upon her as she labored, her lack of nutrition making the venture almost impossible.

After about five minutes, she noticed a man approaching, so Saida stood and watched him. He was roughly dressed in a garment made of camel's hair, a leather belt around his waist. His hair was a clutter of dried-out locks scattered in every direction by the dry desert wind. His skin, like his belt, was leathery and weathered—obviously a man who did not spend much time indoors.

He was a mess. *Just another poor soul trying to sustain himself,* she surmised.

"Good woman," he said as he reached her, "would you be so kind as to bring me a little water in a jar so that I might have a drink?"

She could tell by his accent that he was an Israelite; what she could not comprehend was why he would travel all the way to stricken Zarephath to seek refuge.

"I have some water at home," she said, feeling a degree of pity for the man. "Wait here and I will get you some."

Without waiting for a reply, she turned to her house.

"And one more thing, good woman," she heard the man call out, stopping her, "please bring me a piece of bread."

This stranger has definitely come to the wrong person, she sadly mused. She turned back to him. "I am afraid, sir—and I tell you this as surely as the Lord your God lives—I do not have any bread to give you. All I have left to my name is a handful of flour in a jar and a drop of oil in a jug. In fact, I am here gathering a few sticks to take home and make a meal for myself and my son that we may eat it and then die."

The Hebrew stranger never blinked. "Good woman, do not be afraid. Go home and do as you have said. But first make a small loaf of bread for me from what you have and bring it to me, and then make something for yourself and your son."

Saida stared at the stranger in disbelief. *Did you even hear a word I said?* she felt like screaming at him, but she chose restraint. *I can barely feed myself, let alone you. Are you mad?*

Again, the man was unmoved. "Hear my words, good woman," he said, his voice sure but his tone tender. "This is what the Lord, the God of Israel, says: 'The jar of flour will not be used up and the jug of oil will not run dry until the day the Lord sends rain on the land.' So now, if you feed me first, I give you my word that you and your son will live."

Again, the widow wanted to rage at this audacious Israelite for his selfish cruelty, but she suddenly felt disarmed. No decent man would make such a request when it meant sure death for a mother and her child. Surely, there was more to this stranger than she could see. "Very well then, sir," she found herself saying, as if the words had come to life and made themselves audible by their own power.

She returned to the house slowly, wondering what odd hope this was that so incomprehensibly carried her along. Perhaps the pangs of poverty were emaciating her mind as well as her body. It made no sense, but at the same time, it seemed strangely right. As she removed the last of her food and prepared a tiny piece of bread with which the Israelite could feed himself, she returned to him, the precious final ember of her life nestled in her palm. How she longed to eat it herself but knew that it was not meant for her.

When she reached the Hebrew, she handed the bread to him. He thanked her and ate slowly, never taking his eyes off her, as if examining her to see how she would react. He ate deliberately, savoring the treasured sustenance as he chewed. Saida felt as if he were ridiculing her, mocking her poverty. And yet she felt subdued, refusing to wail at him in fury.

At last, the stranger had finished eating. "You have shown great faith, good woman," he said, the slightest of smiles on his face. "Return now to your home. You will find your jar filled with flour and your jug brimming with olive oil. See for yourself, then come back to me."

What this man said defied every shred of logic she had, and yet somehow she believed him. Saida nodded in affirmation, turned, and walked as quickly as she could. When she reached her door, she stopped, her heart racing with anticipation.

It made no sense whatsoever, and yet...as she approached the table where the jar and jug lay, she looked at them—then fell to the ground, her strength sapped in an instant. She gazed upon the precious pottery, and it was just as the stranger had said. The jar was so full that the flour was running over the side. Same with the oil, as it streaked down the jug and onto the table.

When the shock wore off, she ran to the Hebrew and fell at his feet. "You are a prophet of God," she cried. "What is your name that I may honor you?"

He helped her to her feet. "My name is Elijah, good woman, and I forbid you from ever bowing before me again. I am but a messenger of the God of Israel, and He has sent me to you that you may know Him. Your faith in Him—by feeding me first at the risk of your life and that of your son—will be rewarded."

Later that day, Saida sat at the table with her son and the prophet. The two adults watched with delight as the boy ate heartily. He consumed his bread with abandon, and Saida could no longer contain herself.

She excused herself and walked outside. The fields were still dry and barren, and the darkening skies offered nothing by way of refreshing the land with a few raindrops, let alone a cool breeze. But within her soul, Saida felt unutterable joy. With her belly full and her son's life spared, she felt a surge of hope inhabit and consume her, filling her with a will to live she had not had in years. The God of Israel had come to her in an incomprehensible way, and she would never forsake Him. He had left His mark.

Her life was saved. Her spirit was resuscitated. Her poverty was shattered.

Widow of Zarephath and You

Poverty is demoralizing, miserable, and sometimes, as in the case with the widow of Zarephath, life-threatening. She was literally down to her last meal.

Her circumstances were tragic, and perhaps so are yours.

If you are mired in poverty, you know demoralization, misery, and hopelessness. You have done everything you can to improve your circumstances, but you keep sinking further. You have sought God in prayer, and yet your situation worsens each day.

Will you ever climb out of this pit of poverty? If you take the Scriptures at face value, your answer is yes.

To get the proper perspective on poverty, it is wise to turn to Jesus. What does He say about it? The answer is "plenty," and trusting His words with all your heart, soul, and mind is the key to finding your way out.

Toward the end of His profound "Sermon on the Mount," Jesus said: "Therefore I tell you, do not worry about your life, what you will eat or drink; or about your body, what you will wear. Is not life more important than food, and the body more important than clothes? Look at the birds of the air; they do not sow or reap or store away in barns, and yet your heavenly Father feeds them. Are you not much more valuable than they? Who of you by worrying can add a single hour to his life? ... So do not worry, saying, 'What shall we eat?' or 'What shall we drink?' or 'What shall we wear?' For the pagans run after all these things, and your heavenly Father knows that you need them" (Matthew 6:25–27; 31–32).

This lengthy passage is critical to understanding not necessarily why you are in your impoverished circumstances, but how to cope with them while you are in them and eventually escape.

The key to the passage is Jesus' words, "...and your heavenly Father knows that you need them." When you pray, it is unnecessary to recite to God a laundry list of needs. He knows every need you have *better than you do*. Instead, it is much better to say, "Lord, I am hopeless and helpless without you. I cannot rescue myself from this poverty, but You can. Lord, provide me with my daily needs according to Your promise. And, dear Lord, please take me out of these circumstances in Your perfect timing."

According to His promise in the very next chapter, the Lord assures you that He will *not* be deaf to your plea: "Which of you, if his son asks for bread, will give him a stone? Or if he asks for a fish, will give him a snake? If you then, though you are evil, know how to give good gifts to your children, how much more will your Father in heaven give good gifts to those who ask him!" (Matthew 7:9–11).

In times of distress, it is best to take God at His word. He knows your impoverishment.

Stay faithful and you will soon know His deliverance.

Josiah
Overcoming an Evil Lineage

"Did I do enough, Lord? Did I do enough?"

The question hounded Josiah as he walked atop the walls of Jerusalem, surveying the city below. It was his twenty-seventh birthday, and he wanted to spend it alone. Well, not exactly alone. He had decided to isolate himself from his officials and advisors as he felt an urgent need to spend time with the God He so desired to please.

"Ah, Lord," he cried out, "I have tried so hard. I have done all I could to turn these stubborn people back to you. But has it been enough, Lord?"

As he continued to examine the city, he stopped for a few moments and looked out over one of its marketplaces. "These people, Lord, do they even understand what I have tried to do? Are my efforts really to go unnoticed? Are the hearts of this people really so cold?"

Resuming his walk, Josiah could not escape the weight he felt pressing upon him—the burden of his grandfather Manasseh and his father Amon. He sighed deeply as he considered them, the two evil men who had preceded him as rulers of Judah and had made his job so difficult. He abhorred what they had done to his beloved nation and even hated them, though he never really knew them. He was six when his grandfather died and eight when several "trusted" officials assassinated his father.

But hate them as he may, they were still his flesh and blood, his ancestors, and they carried in them the bloodline of King David, just as he did. And yet they had desecrated David's great name by their shameful actions. "Oh, Lord, is there anything I can do to save my people from the evil perpetrated upon them by my father and grandfather. Am I any better than this evil lineage I have descended from?"

Evil it was. Though the nation of Israel had long been at the mercy of corrupt and sinful monarchs, they had never seen anything like Josiah's grandfather Manasseh. This is saying much considering that Israel was forced to endure twenty-four years of the atrocious reign of the evil king Ahab about two hundred years earlier.

But when it came to sheer wickedness, Ahab had nothing on Manasseh. For fifty-five agonizing years, the twisted monarch plunged the nation into incomprehensible depths of idol worship, wickedness, and depravity, culminating with Manasseh sacrificing his own son to a pagan deity. If this were not enough, Manasseh was also a ruthless tyrant, executing countless innocents who voiced their objections against him.

When at last his five-and-one-half-decade reign of terror was over at age sixty-seven, his son Amon, just twenty-two, succeeded him. If the people thought things would be different, they were wrong. Amon continued the demented practices of his father and threatened to sink the nation even further into its mire of iniquity. But before Amon could take firm grip of the kingdom, his officials murdered him just two years into his reign.

"Oh, Lord," Josiah cried out, falling to his knees, "what kind of darkness has so inhabited these men that they could have committed such evil? What could have possessed them to hate You with such bitterness and revulsion?"

Those who plotted Amon's death were in turn executed, but at least their intentions would be realized. In their desire to purge the nation of its sin, they placed their hopes in the eight-year-old heir whom they prayed would grow up to be a righteous ruler. Josiah's coronation was a blur to the boy. Judah's highest-ranking officials would rule Israel until Josiah grew into the role. In the meantime, his education and upbringing were overseen by his godly mother Jedidah, a rare light shimmering in the darkness of deprivation.

Her efforts paid off wonderfully. When Josiah reached age sixteen, something amazing happened. His heart was suddenly transformed, and he began seeking after the God of Israel. When he was twenty, he put his zeal into action. He ordered a purge of the land from all pagan practices. In a mass sweep of the nation, Josiah personally led his army and officials on a mission to destroy the high places where worshipers burned incense to the sun. He cut down all the Asherah poles—structures designed to help aid in the adoration of the wretched mother-goddess Asherah, whose worship included lewd and degrading sexual practices—and demolished carved idols and cast images.

"And yet, Lord," he said while continuing his turn around the city wall, "was it enough? Was it enough to cleanse Israel of the filth spewed upon it by my father and grandfather?"

Evidently not. At least, not as far as the young king was concerned.

By age twenty-six—the eighteenth year of his reign—he decided to repair the temple of the Lord. After all, if he was going to destroy pagan worship, he had to give his people a better alternative. Because his father and grandfather had allowed the house of God to fall into ruin and neglect, it had become desolate.

"Lord," Josiah declared, "your house will once again become a place of prayer and honor for You." And so the still-youthful king set out to reconstruct not only Israel's house of worship, but also the hearts of the people who had strayed so far from Him.

Then one day, the high priest Hilkiah found the book of Moses.[23] The sacred writings were taken to Josiah. Upon hearing the law of God—and how dismally it had been forsaken—he tore his robes and mourned over his own sin and neglect, as well as that of his people. He sent his officials to the prophetess Huldah to seek God's will. Her words pierced the young monarch's heart. "Great is the Lord's anger that is poured out on us because our fathers have not kept the word of the Lord; they have not acted according to all that is written in the book."

---

[23] The first five books of the Old Testament: Genesis, Exodus, Leviticus, Numbers, and Deuteronomy.

But she also had words of comfort. "The Lord says, 'Tell Josiah this: Because your heart was responsive and you humbled yourself before the Lord when you heard what I have spoken against this place and its people, that they would become accursed and laid waste, and because you tore your robes and wept in my presence, I have heard you, declares the Lord. Therefore I will gather you to your fathers, and you will be buried in peace. Your eyes will not see all the disaster I am going to bring on this place.'"

This was not good enough for Josiah. It was not enough that *only* he be saved, but he sought to save the lives—and souls—of his people. He gathered the entire nation and had the Book of Moses read to them. He renewed God's covenant with Israel and vowed to live by it. He went to places in Israel that were beyond his jurisdiction and purged the idols that still existed. Then he invited his people to attend the most spectacular observance of Passover it had ever seen.

And now Josiah was twenty-seven years old, but he felt much older. He had been king for nineteen years and was beginning to wonder if all his reforms had even made a dent in the hearts of his people. The prophets Jeremiah and Zephaniah were still railing against the people's sin, a sure indication that all his work was purely cosmetic as far as his subjects were concerned.

As he came to the end of his jaunt around Jerusalem's wall, he fell on his face. "Oh, Lord, what was it all worth? If You are still determined to punish this nation for the sins of my grandfather and father, then what good have I done? Am I to forever be attached to their evil, to be included in their wicked heritage? Has anything I done mattered at all, Lord?"

Then, in the quiet of Josiah's heart, God spoke. *"Josiah, my son, I have raised you up from a boy to be the ruler of this people."* God's voice flowed through the troubled king's soul like a gentle breeze following a hailstorm. *"Though you share the blood of your grandfather and father, this is the extent of it. You are not like them. You have overcome their terrible lineage and stand alone as my faithful servant. Continue in your righteous ways, Josiah, and when you are through, you will rest with Me for eternity. Yes, you are the offspring of evil, but you have triumphed gloriously over it. Take heart, Josiah, take heart."*

Renewed as never before, Josiah quickly rose, wiped his eyes, returned to his palace, and called for his closest advisors and administrators.

"Gentlemen," he said boldly, defiantly, and passionately, "we have work to do. This nation may be doomed, but it will not happen on my watch! So long as I live, these people will know that there is a God in Israel!"

Josiah and You

Josiah was among Israel's greatest and most righteous kings.

In fact, depending where you rank David, Josiah was either *the* greatest Israelite king or—at very worst—the second greatest. Though David was famously referred to as a man after God's own heart (1 Samuel 13:14), you'd be pretty safe in saying that Josiah also deserved the "famous" tagline. And yet, despite his greatness, righteousness, and devotion, he was the direct descendant of two vile men—his grandfather Manasseh and his father Amon. These men knew no bounds regarding their sin and were responsible for quickening Israel's judgment. Josiah, however, thrived despite this evil lineage.

But what about you?

If you were fortunate to have loving, caring parents, that's a blessing. However, what if you had evil parents or grandparents? What if you are the direct descendant of those who have perpetrated heinous crimes or have committed ghastly acts?

Does their evil "rub off" on you? In other words, when God sees you, does he see them? The answer, joyfully, is a resounding "no"!

In ancient Israel, the people had a saying that went, "The fathers eat sour grapes, and the children's teeth are set on edge" (Ezekiel 18:1). This means that when fathers sin, children pay the price.

"Wrong!" says the Lord.

Ezekiel continues. "Suppose there is a righteous man who does what is just and right.... He follows my decrees and faithfully keeps my laws. That man is righteous; he will surely live, declares the Sovereign Lord" (Ezekiel 18:3, 9).

So far, so good. Keep reading. "Suppose he has a violent son, who sheds blood...he defiles his neighbor's wife. He oppresses the poor and needy. He commits robbery...Will such a man live? He will not! Because he has done all these detestable things, he will surely be put to death and his blood will be on his own head" (Ezekiel 18:10–13).

Are you seeing a pattern here? Keep reading. "But suppose this son has a son who sees all the sins his father commits, and though he sees them, he does not do such things...he does not defile his neighbor's wife. He does not oppress anyone...he does not commit robbery but gives his food to the hungry and provides clothing for the naked. He withholds his hand from sin...he keeps my laws and follows my decrees. *He will not die for his father's sin; he will surely live*" (Ezekiel 18:14–17, emphasis added).

Yes, the world may look at you and say, "You are the daughter or son of so and so? How terrible."

God, however, sees you and you alone. No matter how wicked a lineage you have descended from, as far as God is concerned, you are an individual for whom Christ died. Family ties mean nothing.

So, do you feel the burden of having been born into an evil family? If so, let it go.

God certainly has!

Daniel

Overcoming Separation

~*~

As Daniel surveyed his circumstances, he just had to laugh. It was not a laugh of irony, nor one of humor. His laughter was one of jubilation. After all, here he was, a man of eighty-two sitting on the floor of an underground prison. He had been thrown into it from a small ceiling opening, and when he hit bottom, he suffered not a scratch, nor felt any pain. Miraculous! Even more miraculous was that he was surround by almost ten lions—starving, food-deprived predators that under any other circumstance would have made a quick meal of their guest.

But Daniel had been with them for twelve hours, and besides a few longing glances, not only had his hosts not laid a paw on him, they also dared not approach. This was because an angel of God was guarding Daniel. From the moment Daniel was so unceremoniously flung into the den, God had dispensed His angel to protect him.

Daniel marveled and laughed jubilantly. The Lord, he realized, was with him now, every bit as much as He was sixty-six years ago when the long decades of Daniel's cruel separation had begun. That was quite a day, Daniel remembered, when he was torn away from his parents at age sixteen. He had no idea then that he would never see them again. And yet the long years had not erased the memory of his parents' faces. He recalled them now as he did then: loving, dignified, courageous. He now understood that they were doing it all for him.

He had spent his final days in Jerusalem during the reign of the wicked king Jehoiakim. The threat of Babylonian invasion hung ominously in the air those days, and when the enemy finally came marching into the holy city, they quickly dispensed with whatever opposition hindered them, then headed straight to the royal palace.

Daniel was prepared. Just one day before, his parents sat him down and told him what would happen. "The Babylonians," his father explained, "will take the brightest and most educated of our young men into exile with them. They will teach you their ways and use you as ambassadors between them and the Jewish captives they will also take with them. Do what they tell you and learn what they teach you."

"I will, Father," Daniel dutifully replied.

"But," his father cautioned, "never forget the God of our ancestors. He will guide you and never leave you. The Babylonians will put tremendous pressure on you to conform, but do not do it. Never turn your back on our glorious God."

Everything happened just as Daniel's father said it would. The Babylonians marched into the royal courts, identified those of noble birth, and separated the children from their parents. As Daniel and his friends Hananiah, Mishael, and Azariah were being led away,

Daniel took one last look back at his parents. They smiled at him. What would be decades of separation had begun.

In Babylon, Daniel and his friends were taught the ways of his new country, so that in three years, they would be fit to serve King Nebuchadnezzar. They were treated well and given the best accommodations in which to live and the best food to eat.

And this is where their first challenge arose. As Daniel and his three companions contemplated the food placed before them on their first day of training, they considered their options. "Friends," Daniel said, "you realize that this food has been offered to idols. For us to eat it would be to honor false gods, something the Mosaic Law will not permit."

"What should we do then?" Hananiah asked.

Daniel had the solution. He persuaded their caretaker to allow them to eat only vegetables and drink water for ten days. If they were not as healthy and well nourished as he desired, then they would eat the king's food. Ten days later, through God's provision, the four Hebrew exiles were the healthiest of the group.

When the training period was completed, Daniel at once distinguished himself and rose to a high position in Nebuchadnezzar's court. He would serve the king faithfully for almost forty years.

Despite his place of honor, Daniel could never feel at home in Babylon. He missed his beloved Jerusalem with a passion and always longed to return. And if that separation was not enough, he had the extra heartache of always being reminded of it. In utter disregard of the high position he had ascended to, he was nonetheless always referred to as "the exile Daniel," "the captive Daniel," "the Jew Daniel." He wore his separation like a cloak, and it remained on him wherever he went.

After many years, the Medo-Persian Empire replaced the Babylonian Empire, and its king, Darius, desired to make Daniel one of the highest-ranking officials of the Babylonian province. This did not sit well with the pagans who did not want to be held accountable to an exiled Jew. They looked for a way to condemn Daniel, but they could find nothing wanting in his character. Therefore, they had to concoct some fraudulent scheme that would allow them to remove him.

"King Darius," they said, "you should issue an edict and enforce the decree that anyone who prays to any god or man during the next thirty days, except to you, O king, shall be thrown into the lions' den."[24]

The plan appealed to the monarch's vanity, so Darius happily ratified it. When Daniel heard of the edict, he was concerned. After all, ever since being taken to Babylon, Daniel had made a practice of praying three times daily at his open upstairs window that faced Jerusalem. Because his window was visible from the street, his actions were evident to the public.

But decree or no decree, Daniel determined that he would not give in. He would continue to pray as he had done for the past six-and-one-half decades. And when he did so for the first time following the

---

[24] Daniel 6:6–8

decree's ratification, he was not surprised to hear troops break into his house, mount the stairs, and rush through his bedroom door.

"Daniel, you of the exiled Hebrews," the commanding officer said, "you are under arrest for disobeying the decree of our great king, Darius. You have been caught praying to one other than him, and for this you must be cast into the lion's den."

The troops moved toward him, but Daniel held up his hand. "No need for handcuffs, gentlemen. I will go with you peacefully."

As he approached the pit that held the famished lions, Daniel was at peace. He knew that no matter what happened in the next few minutes, the Lord had things well under control. When he reached his destination, Daniel was greeted by a distraught Darius.

"Daniel," he king said, almost pleading, "this is a heinous thing indeed. I have been tricked into this by deceptive officials, and, in accordance with the laws of the Medes and the Persians, I cannot appeal your verdict."

He then put his hands on the older gentleman's shoulders. "Daniel, may your God, whom you serve continually, rescue you!"

Daniel hoped to calm the king's anxiety with a smile, but Darius could not be comforted. It was more bitter for him than for Daniel. Daniel then turned and indicated that he was ready to face his sentence.

As the stone was lifted from the small opening designed for dispensing food, Daniel could hear the voracious roars of the lions. If this was to be his fate, he knew it would pass quickly. But before he could ponder any further, he felt himself being grabbed by a burly guard and quickly dispatched into the hole. He fell quickly, striking the ground with a thud. Amazingly, however, he never felt it. As he looked around him, he noticed the lions gazing at him, wanting to pounce but were unable to.

He then sensed a presence behind him and turned. He fell to his face at the sight of the fearsome creature that hovered at his back. When he regained his strength, he crawled to a nearby wall and sat back. Then he wept a weeping of gratitude. The angel would remain until morning, when Daniel would be taken up out of the lion's den.

And now, as the stately old man awaited that moment, he was serene, euphoric. As it turned out, his time in the lion's den had been ecstatic. It had given him the opportunity to reflect on how God had delivered him from all those who sought to destroy him during these many years of separation. But when he considered it more acutely, it occurred to him that never at any time was he ever *really* separated. Not from God, at least.

He had been ripped from his family as a teenager, kidnapped from his beloved city, forced to live in a heathen society, never to return home. But separated? From loved ones? Yes. From his home country? Yes. From his beloved God? Never.

And never would be.

Daniel and You

Separation is difficult.

Daniel experienced it when he was carried away from his family and forced to spend the rest of his life in exile. But though separated, Daniel was never abandoned.

And neither are you.

Have you been separated or feel a sense of separation? Perhaps a job situation has forced you to relocate to a new city. Perhaps a loved one has died, and you feel the pain of earthly separation from that person. Perhaps you have had a falling out with a loved one or family member, and the sting of separation is weighing heavily upon you. You are learning that separation can be a terrible thing.

However, as God's special possession, though you are separate in this world, you are never cast off from Him. There is nowhere you can go or nothing you can experience that can take you away from God. He is there no matter what.

The book of Isaiah offers you these magnificent words: "Even to your old age and gray hairs I am he, I am he who will sustain you. I have made you and I will carry you; I will sustain you and I will rescue you" (Isaiah 46:4). You must admit, these are some pretty overwhelming words.

Note the Lord's loyalty, perseverance, and fortitude. He is utterly determined to stick by you *no matter what!* Age cannot and will not separate you from God. Circumstances cannot and will not separate you from God.

Why is this?

God supplies the answer when He says, "I have made you." You are God's physical creation, as is every person who ever lived. However, as a follower of Jesus Christ, you were created anew spiritually (2 Corinthians 5:17). Therefore, God has pledged Himself to you and has guaranteed you several things. One of them is to "sustain" you. Are you lacking in any area? God is there to provide. He has promised to carry you. Are you weak physically, emotionally, or spiritually? The Lord is there to enable you to "soar on wings like eagles" (Isaiah 40:31).

God has also committed himself to "rescue" you. Are you in danger? Consider this. Before coming to know Christ, your soul was in danger. However, upon receiving Christ, God rescued you from an eternity separated from Him. But what about in this life? Are you in danger of affliction, death, or not being able to meet your financial needs? God is there to rescue you.

Are you lonely and far from home physically? Separate and cast off emotionally? Distant and downcast spiritually? Are the passing years weighing on you as you age?

Rest peacefully. God is with you.

You may feel separate from God, but He has not separated Himself from you. He will help you overcome your sense of separation as well as triumph over it.

So whatever you do, never despair. And never forget that even to your old age and gray hairs, He is God! Your God! No matter what.

Nehemiah

OVERCOMING OPPOSITION

The great work was over.

The walls of Jerusalem had been rebuilt. It had taken fifty-two days. To Nehemiah, it seemed much longer. The brutal opposition he and his fellow builders faced was the biggest challenge of his life. There were times when he did not think he was going to make it.

But he did. And Nehemiah stood amazed. "Oh, Lord," he said, falling to his knees after surveying the walls, "You have done an amazing work. These stones live again. This wall is alive! You have taken what was dead and breathed Your life back into it. Without You, Lord…"

But Nehemiah could not finish. The project—and the fierce resistance it faced—had drained him of his strength, but not his gratitude. As he looked upon the glorious walls, he felt a surge of pride, joy, and wonder.

It had been nine months since a contingent from Jerusalem—led by his brother Hanani—had come to visit him in Persia. Nehemiah was a court official, the cupbearer for King Artaxerxes.

The news they delivered was dire. "Our people in Jerusalem and Judah are in great trouble and disgrace. The wall of Jerusalem is broken down, and its gates have been burned with fire."[25]

Nehemiah felt his knees go weak. He found a chair and sat. "This is grave news," he told Hanani. "How did this happen?"

"Sanballat from Horon, the governor of Samaria, hates our people and seeks our destruction," Hanani said. "He would rule over all Judea if he could, but the king has not given him such power."

"Praise God for that," Nehemiah surmised.

"Sanballat does not work alone, Nehemiah. Wherever he goes, he is followed by two officials—Tobiah from Ammon and an Arab official named Geshem. I have no doubt they are behind the destruction of the walls and have set them on fire. They are persistent, Nehemiah, and they plague our people."

"This news distresses me beyond words, Hanani. I am deeply saddened by it."

"Then pray about it, my brother, and use your influence with the king. Perhaps the Lord will fight for us and rebuild our walls and gates."

Nehemiah did what his brother asked. He prayed fervently—for fourth months—before voicing his distress to Artaxerxes. Not only did he seek a lengthy absence from his court duties to return to Jerusalem to help repair the walls, but he also asked the king to give

---

[25] Nehemiah 1:3

him papers assuring his safety on the almost thousand-mile trip that would take him three months to complete.

Nehemiah found breathing difficult as the king sat back on his throne and pondered his trusted official's request. Nehemiah never stopped silently praying. Artaxerxes looked up. "Nehemiah," he said in his most regal tone, "I now appoint you as governor of Jerusalem. You will return at once to your homeland and do all the work your God has put in your heart to do. I will provide you with whatever you need."

The first battle was won, but the war ahead would be overwhelming. "Lord," Nehemiah prayed as he set out, "if You forsake me for but a second, I cannot stand. Strengthen me, Lord, to do this work which You have ordained."

With the trip at last completed, Nehemiah made his presence known to but several officials. After three days in Jerusalem, he set out by horse at night with a few men to inspect the wall. He surveyed it from every angle—and was mortified. "Oh, Lord," he said, "the rubble alone is a massive obstacle. Removing it will rob the men of their strength."

He quickly regained his resolve. "No, Lord! I will not give in to discouragement. You have laid this task at my feet, and in Your strength, I will work until the final stone is set in place!"

The next day, Nehemiah gathered the officials of Judah, along with the priests, Levites, and men and women. "You see the trouble we are in," he told them. "Jerusalem lies in ruins, and its gates have been burned with fire. Come, let us rebuild the wall of Jerusalem, and we will no longer be in disgrace."[26]

The rest of the day was spent making plans—who would build what sections of the wall and what each man's, woman's, and child's responsibility would be. The following morning, the people arrived early, excited, and ready to work. But they were not alone.

"I see we have company," Nehemiah told Hanani.

"I knew this would happen. Sanballat wants to intimidate us. He has brought with him the army of Samaria."

"Not a very impressive army," Nehemiah, who had seen the Persian forces, concluded.

"No," Hanani agreed, "but they are impressive enough to frighten our people."

Nehemiah climbed a large pile of rubble. "People of Judah and Jerusalem," he roared. "Today, we will begin a great work for the God of our fathers. It is He we serve. Pay no attention to the opposition surrounding us. It is the Lord who fights for us. Be courageous and work with all your hearts."

Which is exactly what the people did—until the taunting began. "Ha!" Sanballat shouted to his officials, loud enough for the builders to hear. "What are those feeble Jews doing? Will they restore their wall? Will they offer sacrifices? Will they finish in a day? Can they bring the stones back to life from those heaps of rubble—burned as they are?"[27]

---

[26] Nehemiah 2:17

[27] Nehemiah 4:2

The officials laughed, and the Jewish builders faltered. "What they are building," Tobiah oafishly added, "if even a fox climbed up on it, he would break down their wall of stones!"[28]

"Pay no attention to such empty words!" Nehemiah implored his people. "You do a noble work. Ignore these men and set your backs to your responsibilities!"

He turned toward his tormentors. "Leave us, Sanballat!" he ordered. "You have no place here! We are engaged in a great endeavor for our God—and we will succeed!"

Sanballat laughed and ordered his forces to retreat. But they came back the next day, and the next and the next. They would be there every day of the great construction project. But Nehemiah prayed, prayed some more, then prayed again. "Hear us, O God, for we are despised. Turn their insults back on their own heads."[29]

And the Lord *did* hear.

The Hebrews worked and the wall grew—from the Sheep Gate to the Fish Gate to the Jeshanah Gate to the Valley Gate to the Dung Gate to the Fountain Gate to the Horse Gate. Israel's former glory was returning! Day by day, the wall rose and its gaps were filled.

And all along, the dark opposition kept coming. Sanballat and his hordes threatened to go to war with the builders and tear down their work. Nehemiah would not be tyrannized. He stationed men with their swords, spears, and bows behind the lowest points of the wall at the exposed places. "Do not be afraid of them," he bellowed.

---

[28] Nehemiah 4:3

[29] Nehemiah 4:4

"Remember the Lord, who is great and awesome, and fight for your brothers, your sons and your daughters, your wives and your homes."[30]

Sanballat grew desperate. He conspired with Israel's false prophets and ordered them to foretell destruction against Nehemiah and Jerusalem. He even turned some Jewish citizens into spies and had them report to him all Nehemiah had said and done. He went as far as to accuse Nehemiah of plotting to set himself up as king of Judah, and then rebelling against the Persian government.

But Nehemiah never gave in; he overcame every one of Sanballat's nefarious plots. Yes, he occasionally flinched, but only in private, and before the Lord. "Oh, God of Israel," he prayed with tears and heartache, "the people's will is weakening. If You forsake us, we will crumble. But Lord, You will never forsake us. Strengthen me, Lord, and strengthen our people."

And then, after fifty-two days, the final gate was set in place. It was finished. Gloriously finished! Sanballat, his officials, and army looked on in shocked silence and rage. Their faces were ashen and their spirits destroyed.

"Away!" Sanballat gave the order, and suddenly, Nehemiah and the men, women, and children of Judah and Jerusalem were alone. They looked at each other, and then at the wall they had rebuilt.

Then, as if guided by one spirit, they erupted in a euphoric explosion of rejoicing that rocked the hills around the great city.

---

[30] Nehemiah 4:14

They danced. They embraced. They wept. They thanked God. They laughed and smiled and exulted.

But Nehemiah did none of those things. These fifty-two days had taken a toll on him. He had led his people and fought the opposition. And he did it all with prayer—endless, desperate prayer. Answered prayer.

And he prayed now. "Oh, Lord, what you have done is marvelous. You have defeated Your enemies and brought glory to Yourself. May your Name be ever exalted!"

He then rose and looked out over the walls of Jerusalem.

It was a beautiful sight indeed.

Nehemiah and You

God commissioned Nehemiah to rebuild Jerusalem's wall (Nehemiah 2:12), and yet he still experienced great opposition. If God gave Nehemiah the project to do, why didn't God remove all obstacles?

What about you?

Has God given you a job to do, but things have not gone as expected? Does it seem that everywhere you turn you face frustration and opposition, if not by men, then certainly from Satan?

Has God led you to teach a Sunday school class, but only one person showed up? Has He given you a heart to evangelize in your workplace, but no one has come to Christ? Has he put you in charge of fundraising for a worthy project, but the funds are not coming in?

"Lord," you pray, "I am doing exactly what You told me to do, but nothing is happening. In fact, all I do is face opposition and defeat."

Take heart and consider the prophet Isaiah. God commanded him, "Go and tell this people: 'Be ever hearing, but never understanding; be ever seeing, but never perceiving' (Isaiah 6:9). In essence, God told Isaiah, "Go and preach My word to the Children of Israel—but they won't listen to you." Huh? What kind of way is *that* to begin a ministry?

And yet God's commission to Isaiah was no less exacting than to someone whose ministry will lead to the salvation of 10,000 people.

So, how do you know whether your commission will be fruitless, like Isaiah's; wonderfully rewarding, like a pastor who builds a church from thirty members to three thousand; or fraught with opposition, as was Nehemiah's?

You don't. But that's not the point. The point is that you do what God wants you to do, and let Him provide the spark you need to carry it out—even in the face of frustration and fierce opposition. Let the words He spoke to ancient Israel encourage you: "Be strong and courageous. Do not be afraid or terrified because of them, for the Lord your God goes with you; he will never leave you nor forsake you" (Deuteronomy 31:6). Notice how the Lord does not guarantee earthly success, but *does* assure that He will be with you despite opposition and seeming failure.

Don't forget that God judges success differently than you do. In Nehemiah's case, success meant the rebuilding of the wall. That was easy to measure. For you, the success of teaching a Sunday school class is based on a healthy attendance. For God, however, success may be one person showing up—and you reaching to that person.

Satan will always oppose God's work. After all, he "prowls around like a roaring lion looking for someone to devour" (1 Peter 5:8). If you are doing God's work, that "someone" is you!

But never ever forget: Even if the whole world turns against you, God never will. Like He said, "he will never leave you nor forsake you."

Frustration? Opposition?

They didn't stop Nehemiah. And with God fighting for you, they won't stop you. So focus on the task and leave the results to God!

Job

Overcoming Great Suffering

―«»→

The ash heaps among which the lepers dwelt were almost desolate but for the presence of Job and his friends Eliphaz, Bildad, and Zophar.

They had sat together for seven days without speaking. Job was there even longer. His body was riddled with oozing, gaping sores from head to foot, and a foul odor was emanating from him. The stench was so great that it sent even the lepers scurrying far away from him.

Job sat day and night, scraping himself with a shard of pottery, marring his already disfigured person even further. All his three friends could do for one endless week was to sit silently, commiserating with him but unable to comfort him.

For Job, who was blameless and upright, fearing God and shunning evil, the news hit in waves of soul-crushing redundancy while he sat at his home squaring his business accounts. He was a wealthy man who owned seven thousand sheep, five hundred yokes of oxen, five hundred donkeys, and a large number of servants. He and his wife were blessed with seven sons and three daughters. And then came the onslaught.

"Sir," a servant cried while bursting into his study, "the oxen were plowing and the donkeys were grazing nearby, and the Sabeans attacked and carried them off. They put the servants to the sword, and I am the only one who has escaped to tell you!"

Before Job could process the implausible account, in ran another servant. His message: fire had come from the sky and killed all the sheep and another huge number of servants. A third servant entered. His message: three raiding parties of Chaldeans stole the camels and killed even more servants. Then came a fourth courier. His pulverizing dispatch: while all ten of Job's children were feasting together, a great desert wind struck the house they were in, destroyed it, and killed them all.

As Job considered the string of devastating reports, he fell to the ground and wailed. When his tears were depleted, he rose, tore his clothes, and shaved his head in mourning and then ... worshiped.

"Naked I came from my mother's womb, and naked I will depart," he groaned. "The Lord gave and the Lord has taken away; may the name of the Lord be praised."

As he rose, he was startled to see his wife, her face white, fear enveloping her. "What has happened?" she asked trembling.

Job communicated the impossible news, then carried her into the house after she collapsed. He spent the next two days consoling her, anguish robbing both of sleep, except when overcome by exhaustion. And then, on the third day, Job awoke to excruciating pain after a brief slumber. He examined himself and noticed that he had been afflicted with some vile disease that had ravished his body with hideous lesions and boils. Grabbing a shard of pottery, he headed to the heap of lepers and began scraping himself. His wife went to the heap, and in her wretched misery, appealed to him, "Are you still holding on to your integrity? Curse God and die!"

Her great suffering had robbed her of hope. But Job was not quite there yet. "You are talking like a foolish woman," he quietly rebuked her. "Shall we accept good from God, and not trouble?"

Now alone, Job descended into a mire and searing misery. "My children. My darling daughters. My beloved sons. My babies."

As each day passed, the horror of what had befallen him began to chisel away at his sanity, faith, and reason. He plunged further into misery by the hour until he was inundated by an all-consuming despair. He hardly noticed when his three friends came and sat silently with him, sharing his wretchedness. And finally, Job poured out his sorrow to God. "Why did I not perish at birth, and die as I came from the womb? For now I would be lying down in peace; I would be asleep and at rest."

He scraped himself some more. "What I feared has come upon me; what I dreaded has happened to me. I have no peace, no quietness; I have no rest, but only turmoil."

His friends, however, saw it differently.

"Consider now: Who, being innocent, has ever perished?" Eliphaz surmised, much to Job's horror. "Where were the upright ever destroyed? As I have observed, those who plow evil and those who sow trouble reap it."

"You think these things have come upon me because of sin I have committed?" Job disdainfully fired back. "You are wrong!"

But Bildad did not concur with Job. "Does God pervert justice?" he viciously attacked. "Does the Almighty pervert what is right? When your children sinned against him, he gave them over to the penalty of their sin."

"Have you just said that my children deserved death because of their wickedness?" Job asked incredulously. "You speak lies!"

Finding no comfort in his friends, Job directed his fury at God. "Even if I summoned him and he responded, I do not believe he would give me a hearing," Job lamented. "He would crush me with a storm and multiply my wounds for no reason. He would not let me regain my breath but would overwhelm me with misery."

And yet, in his burning torment and madness, he still held on to a trace of faith. "Though he slay me, yet I will hope in him," Job declared. "He knows the way I take; when he has tested me, I will come forth as gold."

Job simply did not comprehend. It was up to Eliphaz to enlighten him. "Is it for your piety that he rebukes you and brings charges against you? Is not your wickedness great? Are not your sins endless? This is why snares are all around you, why sudden peril terrifies you."

Thinking that his friends were a lost cause, Job continued his slide into wretchedness by continuing to accuse the Lord. "Withdraw your hand far from me, and stop frightening me with your terrors." Job was convinced that he was right in all things while his friends—and even God—were wrong. "I will never admit you are in the right; till I die, I will not deny my integrity," he proclaimed to his accusers. "I will maintain my righteousness and never let go of it; my conscience will not reproach me as long as I live."

Suddenly, the sky grew dark and cloudy, and a terrible storm kicked up in an instant. The four petrified men cowered in fright and sought to flee, but they were paralyzed by overwhelming fear.

"Who is this that darkens my counsel with words without knowledge?" the Lord thundered in dreadful glory and power. "Brace yourself like a man, Job; I will question you, and you shall answer me."

Time had vanished. Heartache, suffering and pain were as nothing. There was only the harrowing and awful voice of the Lord. "Where were you when I laid the earth's foundation? Tell me, if you understand! Who shut up the sea behind doors when it burst forth from the womb? Have you journeyed to the springs of the sea or walked in the recesses of the deep? Can you bind the beautiful Pleiades? Can you loose the cords of Orion? Will the one who contends with the Almighty correct him? Let him who accuses God answer him!"

Job had demanded an audience with God. He received it and was devastated by what he saw and heard. "Surely I spoke of things I did not understand, things too wonderful for me to know," Job confessed, his face pressed to the ground. "My ears had heard of you but now my eyes have seen you. Therefore I despise myself and repent in dust and ashes."

In an instant, the storm was over, replaced by a wondrous ray of light and God's unfathomable forgiveness and healing.

Over the years, the Lord would restore to Job double of what he lost, including three more daughters and seven more sons. His life would be long and prosperous, his great suffering tempered, diminished, and eventually obliterated. And Job would never question God again. He never would find out why tragedy had befallen him, but as the years passed, it hardly mattered. He had come to a deeper sense of the majesty and loving care of God and had learned to fully trust him.

In the end, God had revealed Himself to Job in a mighty and most unlikely way.

"Oh, Lord," Job cried out in his old age, "you have upheld me during my great suffering. You have restored my great losses. You have redeemed a soul buried in despair. Your ways are exalted and beyond knowing. All your ways are perfect. May nothing but praise ever come from my lips again!"

Job and You

Job's despair was acute. Who can blame him for crying out, "And now my life ebbs away; days of suffering grip me" (Job 30:16).

Perhaps you understand Job's pain. Perhaps you have suffered tremendous loss and feel you cannot go on. Perhaps you have lost a loved one, even a child, and pain haunts your every waking second.

It is a terrible and tragic weight to bear. But your great consolation is this: you don't carry your suffering alone. In your great pain, Job speaks to you and says, "But those who suffer [God] delivers in their suffering; he speaks to them in their affliction" (Job 36:15).

If you know Jesus Christ as your Lord and Savior, be assured that He is there. You are not left to carry your suffering in isolation. Though you must endure the grieving process, note how God quickens that process. Job says, "But those who suffer he delivers in their suffering." In other words, God does not wait for the human process—which could take years—to do its work, but is delivering you while you suffer. God was there the second your suffering began. He is there in the midst of it. And not only will He be there at the end of it, but He will hasten the end as He delivers healing to your bruised and shattered soul.

Another consideration to aid you in your suffering is to remember that though some suffering comes from God as a means of discipline (Isaiah 38:17), very often your suffering has nothing whatsoever to do with any wrong act you have committed. It simply happened because the world is evil and under the curse of sin. And though suffering is painful—sometimes unbearably so—keep in mind that there is at least one notable benefit of it: Christlikeness. "For it has been granted to you on behalf of Christ not only to believe on him, but also to suffer for him..." (Philippians 1:29). Granted, this verse specifically refers to suffering because of faith (as in persecution), but in a general sense, it does speak to the overall fellowship you share with Christ in the suffering He endured when He died on the cross.

Regardless of the reason for your suffering, you can be assured that God is always with you in the midst of it. The apostle Paul says, "For just as the sufferings of Christ flow over into our lives, so also through Christ our comfort overflows" (2 Corinthians 1:5). As a Christian, your suffering is automatically and immediately accompanied by God's comfort. God does not allow you to suffer apart from His comfort. Even when the pain is so great that you are unable to feel anything else, be assured that God is dispensing comfort to you even as your heart breaks.

So, if you are experiencing terrible sorrow, you will overcome it! God is with you, and in time, "You will surely forget your trouble, recalling it only as waters gone by" (Job 11:16).

Hosea

OVERCOMING AN ADULTERESS MARRIAGE

←«»→

In his forty-two years, Hosea had never been to the Samaritan slave market.

And now, as we snaked his way through its crowded streets, he felt dirty, contaminated, unholy. *Oh, Gomer,* he cried silently over his fallen wife, *how could your path have possibly led you to this place?*

Feeling overcome, Hosea found an empty stool near a food vendor's stall and sat down. He needed time to regain his wits—and to think back ten years to when this tragedy all began.

It had been a particularly trying day for the then thirty-two-year-old prophet. "Hear the word of the Lord, you Israelites," he boomed in the courtyards of the temple of Samaria, the capital of Israel's northern kingdom. "The Lord has a charge to bring against you who live in the land: 'There is no faithfulness, no love, no acknowledgment of God in the land. There is only cursing, lying and murder, stealing and adultery; they break all bounds, and bloodshed follows bloodshed."[31]

The Israelites scurried like insects when the thunderous prophet hurled the Lord's condemnation at them, running as fast as they could to flee his voracious denunciations. As Hosea left the pagan temple, he felt the burden and loneliness of God's call upon him. He needed time with God, so he retreated to the hills just outside his home, the place where he could pour his heart out to the Lord and receive comfort in return.

"Oh, Lord, the weight you have placed on me his heavy. Though I honor your call, Lord, I so desire your peace."

"Hosea," the Lord answered within the quiet of the prophet's soul, "take to yourself an adulterous wife and children of unfaithfulness, because the land is guilty of the vilest adultery in departing from the Lord."[32]

The prophet froze, dumbfounded by what he had just heard. He waited to hear more, but the Lord was silent. God had made His will clear. It took a day for Hosea to try to figure out what the Lord said but knew that obedience must supersede his confusion. Two days later, he visited a neighbor, a farmer by the name of Diblaim. He had often approached the prophet, pleading with him to marry his beautiful daughter, Gomer. "I know she is somewhat simple and unsteady, but is she not beautiful, man of God?" Diblaim touted, trying to make the sale. "She will provide you with sons—many of them."

---

[31] Hosea 4:1–2
[32] Hosea 1:2

Diblaim was right about one thing—at age seventeen, Gomer was indeed beautiful. Arrangements were made that week and a betrothal was entered into. Over the next year, Hosea and Gomer spent most evenings together getting to know each other. Gomer *was* rather simple but also youthful, warm, and full of life. And against every instinct he had, knowing what lay ahead, Hosea fell in love with her.

The first year of marriage was wonderful. The second was more challenging. "Husband," Gomer said to him one night, "why do the people hate you as they do?"

"I speak the truth to them, and they do not want to hear it."

"Must you always speak so?"

"I must speak whatever the Lord tells me to speak."

"But..."

"What is wrong, Gomer? Why such questions? You know that I have been called by God for such a mission."

"I know, dear husband, but it is just that the people have started to ridicule me in the marketplace."

Hosea was irate. "Who, Gomer? Who dares insult you?"

"No one I can identify. I hear their taunts from a distance."

"Nonetheless, Gomer, I cannot stop speaking the word of the Lord. Perhaps Hoglah can begin doing the shopping for us. She is a reliable servant; we can certainly depend on her."

"But husband, I love going to the marketplace."

Over the next few months, the situation worsened. "Hosea," Gomer would complain, "I do not understand this God of yours at all. Does He *want* to make my life miserable? Does He take joy in tormenting me?"

Hosea tried explaining, but Gomer did not want to hear. In the third year of their marriage, Gomer became pregnant. The couple's first child was a boy. "The Lord has commanded me to name him Jezreel," Hosea proclaimed.

"What sort of name is this?" Gomer objected. "It is the name of a city. It makes no sense."

"Nonetheless, my love, God has a purpose. The child's name symbolizes Israel's sin."

Gomer still did not understand. During their fourth year of marriage, the couple was drifting further and further apart. Disturbing rumors were beginning to circulate about Gomer. She had been seen entering another man's home while Hosea preached. He buried the words deep in his consciousness.

In their fifth year of marriage, Gomer again became pregnant. The couple welcomed a beautiful girl to their family. "The Lord has ordained that we call her Lo-Ruhamah," Hosea declared.

"Lo-Ruhamah?" Gomer puzzled. "'Not loved?' But this is preposterous, my husband. Look at her, Hosea? How can you name this precious child 'Not Loved'?"

Hosea knew that an explanation would be futile.

By year six, the marriage was all but dead, and yet the prophet still loved his straying wife. Year seven saw the birth of a third child. "The Lord has named him Lo-Ammi, for, says the Lord to Israel, 'you are not my people, and I am not your God.'"[33]

---

[33] Hosea 1:8

Gomer's eyes were cold and unblinking. "Nor is your God my God, Hosea."

Gomer came to detest her husband and his God. In the eighth year, Hosea returned home one day and was greeted by their servant. "Sir," Hoglah said with tears streaming, "Gomer is gone."

"What do you mean?"

"She told me that she is leaving and will never return to you. That life with you …"

"Please, Hoglah, feel free to speak."

"That life with you is unbearable."

Hosea sat down, overcome. "But perhaps," Hoglah ventured, "it is for the best."

"How can you say such a thing, woman?"

"Well, sir, I mean, you know what she has been like."

"What are you talking about, Hoglah?"

"Oh, sir, you have blinded yourself to the truth! Could you not see that though your oldest child bears a striking resemblance to you, your two youngest look nothing like you? Have you never noticed that, sir?"

Yes, he knew it, and knew it well. The next year was misery for Hosea, his only solace being Hoglah, who served as a mother to the children. He had no idea what he would have done without her.

Then, two years following Gomer's departure, Hosea heard a knock on the door. It was a woman. "Sir," she said nervously. "I come with news of your wife."

"Who are you?"

"The daughter of the last man she lived with."

Hosea shuddered and invited her in. "Your wife has been living with us for a month as a servant."

"Where?"

"In Jezreel."

"Before that, she had been serving as a shrine prostitute in the temple…"

Hosea felt his soul shatter. "One day, she begged my father—a frequent visitor to the temple—to take her away from such a life. She offered to become a servant in our house. My father agreed, but sadly she proved inept, and we could no longer keep her. My father suggested she return home. The morning she left us, I asked her where she was going."

"What did she say?"

"She told me that she was the wife of the prophet Hosea—which shocked me—but that you would never accept her back." Hosea was on the verge of tears. "She told me that she would offer herself in the Samaria slave market to anyone who would have her. She desired to be taken far from Israel."

That night, Hosea prayed, and God responded, "Go, show your love to your wife again, though she is loved by another and is an adulteress. Love her as the Lord loves the Israelites."[34]

---

[34] Hosea 3:1

Now, in the slave market, as the bidding began, Hosea looked up at Gomer, the first time he had seen her in twenty-four months. She looked far older than her twenty-seven years.

Hosea was the only bidder. "I will give fifteen shekels of silver and fifteen shekels worth of barley for this woman."

Hosea looked at Gomer and she at him. She trembled and looked away. The transaction was made. Gomer stood alone, near naked, and shivering in the cold. Hosea's heart pounded as he approached her. Gomer still could not look at him. Hosea removed his outer garment and placed it around her. "Let us go home, Gomer."

His arm cradling her ever so tenderly, he accompanied his trembling bride back to their home and children. It would take years to heal, he knew, but he was certain they would do so. Eventually. They would overcome the terrible adultery that had crushed them both.

They would overcome with love: Hosea's love for Gomer; Gomer's rekindled love for the husband who redeemed her; God's love for these two tormented souls.

Hosea and You

Adultery is one of the most crushing forms of betrayal a person can face. What must Hosea have thought when God commanded him to marry a woman who would eventually commit adultery? How horrible was it for him—despite knowing what would happen—to live through it?

What about you? Have you lived with an adulterous spouse? Have you committed adultery?

If so, can God forgive? Can He restore? Can you ever be the same again? The answer, wonderfully, is yes on all counts!

At the conclusion of the book of Hosea, God promises restoration to Israel, which had committed spiritual adultery against Him by worshiping idols. Despite their terrible sin, God told them, "Return, O Israel, to the Lord your God. Your sins have been your downfall! Take words with you and return to the Lord. Say to him: 'Forgive all our sins and receive us graciously, that we may offer the fruit of our lips'" (Hosea 14:1–2).

If you have committed adultery, notice the first step: repentance. You must ask God to forgive you. "But," you say, "how can I possibly seek God's forgiveness after what I have done? Will he even listen to me?"

God's reply to Israel is your answer. "I will heal their waywardness and love them freely, for my anger has turned away from them. I will be like the dew to Israel; he will blossom like a lily" (Hosea 1:4–5). God *always* forgives the contrite heart, but He doesn't stop there. He promises to help you bloom and flourish again, just like a flower.

The key to understanding God's forgiveness and restoration is to comprehend His nature. The prophet Daniel tells us that, "The Lord our God is merciful and forgiving, even though we have rebelled against him" (Daniel 9:9). In other words, our actions cannot change God's character. By nature, He is merciful and forgiving—even if we are guilty of vile sins. Have you committed adultery? There will be consequences, but being forever separated from God *is not* one of them. Your repentance is all that is required to gain access back into His favor.

What if your spouse has committed adultery? Its pain was devastating and perhaps you still feel the brunt of it. Will you ever regain your strength to become the person you once were? Psalm 71:20 says yes. "Though you have made me see troubles, many and bitter, you will restore my life again; from the depths of the earth you will again bring me up."

Gloom and dreariness cannot separate you from God. Despair and emotional upheaval are no hindrances to Him. Do you feel as if you have been cast down to the "depths of the earth?"

Don't give up. If adultery has been a part of your life, you are not without hope. Far from it. Commit yourself to God's care and He *will* eventually lift you up.

With God, you can and will overcome the crushing pain of adultery.

Elizabeth

Overcoming Hopelessness

←«»→

Elizabeth giggled as she kissed Zechariah on the forehead. She felt like a mother sending her little boy off to school at the local synagogue. Except that Elizabeth was fifty-one and her husband was nearing sixty. "This is your day," she said to him, sharing his joy.

"Oh, Elizabeth, I have awaited it for decades."

"I will be thinking of you."

They shared a quick kiss, and Zechariah began traversing the hills of Judea to nearby Jerusalem.

It was indeed Zechariah's day, the only time in his life when he would be bestowed with the opportunity to offer incense to the Lord in the great temple. To Elizabeth, Zechariah was well deserving of the honor, a marvelous reward for a lifetime of faithful service in Israel's priesthood.

As Elizabeth watched him ride atop his donkey, the image of a mother sending her boy off to school returned. As a girl, Elizabeth remembered standing with her own mother as she sent Elizabeth's brothers off to the synagogue to receive their education. Elizabeth dreamed of the day when she, too, would do the same for her sons.

She dreamed of it at age fifteen when this beautiful priest's daughter married a twenty-four-year-old son of a priest, and hopes of a large and bustling family shone in the bright future.

Elizabeth dreamed about it five years later when there should have been two or three young ones running around the house. She had not conceived yet but still had hope.

Elizabeth continued to dream about it ten years into their marriage when she still possessed the hope that youth encouraged, though there was still no conception.

By age thirty, Elizabeth still dreamed of sending her sons off to school, but not quite as wistfully as she had done in her twenties. By age thirty-five, Elizabeth had stopped dreaming, though she still continued to hope. However, by her mid-forties, hope had died. Her body was no longer capable of producing children.

The day she accepted this reality, she cried quietly. When Zechariah wondered why she wept, she simply looked at him with tears streaming down her face. It took him a few seconds, but he figured it out. "May the Lord's will be done," he said tenderly. "I would not trade you for the most fertile woman in all of Judea."

It was the most wonderful thing he could have said, but it did not take away the pain. Nor the shame. Though loved by her neighbors, Elizabeth knew exactly what they thought: someway and somehow, this couple must have sinned terribly for the Lord to curse them with barrenness.

Elizabeth would carry her infertility with dignity. *That* she could do. What was difficult to bear was the hopelessness of it all. For the first thirty years of their marriage, so long as her body was capable, at least there was hope. True, it dwindled over the years, but an ember of it still burned. But when her life change came, she knew it was over. Her hope for children was dead, and she profoundly felt the terrible shame and emptiness of it.

But for right now, there were things to do. Elizabeth had clothes to wash and bread to bake, activities that would occupy her well into the early hours of the afternoon. She was grateful for the distraction these chores provided and set herself to do them well. Her early morning musings aside now, the day passed quickly. It was certainly unspectacular but productive, and Elizabeth could ask for nothing more.

So she thought. Suddenly, as she finished wrapping some newly baked loaves of bread in cloth, she was startled when Zechariah came crashing through the door. Elizabeth ran to him. "What is wrong? Did something happen at the temple?"

He pointed to his ears. Elizabeth was baffled. "I do not understand."

Zechariah gazed at her intently, urging her to pay attention. He again pointed to his ears and nodded negatively. He then pointed to his lips and did the same. Elizabeth struggled to comprehend, so Zechariah repeated his strange behavior. It finally dawned on her. "You cannot hear or speak, is this what you are telling me, husband?"

He nodded affirmatively. Elizabeth was alarmed. "Has something terrible happened?"

Zechariah gripped her firmly by the shoulders, smiled widely, and again nodded negatively. Then, amazingly, he looked down at her belly and patted it. Elizabeth stepped back, as if Zechariah had tried to bite her. "What has gotten into you, husband? I have never seen you act in such a way."

Zechariah held up his hands to calm her, then indicated to her that she should remain where she was for a few moments. Elizabeth watched as Zechariah hurried to their bedroom then returned with a piece of papyrus and a reed pen. He spread the sheet on a table and indicated to Elizabeth that she should sit next to him. She did so—warily. He began to write. "This morning, as I was burning incense in the Holy Place, an angel appeared to me."

Elizabeth looked at Zechariah wide-eyed. He resumed writing. "He was fearsome and I felt I would faint." Zechariah looked at his wife to make sure she was following. She nodded. "The angel strengthened me, then spoke. He said, 'Do not be afraid, Zechariah; your prayer has been heard. Your wife Elizabeth will bear you a son, and you are to call him John.'"[35]

---

[35] Luke 1:13

As Elizabeth read the impossible words, she felt a chill. She quickly rose from the table and ran to another side of the room. But before she could get any further, Zechariah grabbed her and forcefully turned her toward him. He pointed to the table and ordered her to return.

Elizabeth had never seen him act so strangely. She knew not to disobey again. Once she was seated, Zechariah calmed himself and urged her to pay attention as he wrote. "The angel said, 'He will be a joy and delight to you, and many will rejoice because of his birth, for he will be great in the sight of the Lord. He will go on before the Lord, in the spirit and power of Elijah, to turn the hearts of the parents to their children and the disobedient to the wisdom of the righteous—to make ready a people prepared for the Lord.'"[36]

Elizabeth could barely control her breathing as her eyes bulged at the incredible words. John comforted her and wrote again. "I did not believe it either, my love. When I expressed my unbelief, the angel said, 'I am Gabriel. I stand in the presence of God, and I have been sent to speak to you and to tell you this good news. And now you will be silent and not able to speak until the day this happens, because you did not believe my words, which will come true at their appointed time.'[37] This is why I can neither speak nor hear."

---

[36] Luke 1:14–15, 17
[37] Luke 1:19–20

Elizabeth looked deeply into her husband's eyes and knew this was not the raving of a madman. His conviction was proof of that. But even beyond this, the look of tenderness, love, and compassion in his eyes was enough to convince her. He wrote again. "Yes, my love, you *are* to become a mother. You *will* have a son."

And, as it all sank in, a wave of gratitude and emotion flooded over Elizabeth, the likes of which she had never experienced. She wanted to thank God in gushing words but speech failed her. She began sobbing uncontrollably, her body heaving in glorious celebration. Zechariah held her, and she began to settle herself.

That night, Zechariah and Elizabeth shared their love. Soon after, the miracle happened. When Elizabeth was certain of her pregnancy, she approached her husband. Trembling, she pointed to her stomach and nodded affirmatively. He began to weep, kneel at her belly, and wrap his arms around her. She returned his embrace. "The Lord has done this for me," she exulted. "In these days, he has shown his favor and taken away my disgrace among the people."[38]

Nine months later, the child was born, and the residents of the hill country of Judea rejoiced for a week. Eight days following the birth, the child John was circumcised, and the Lord restored Zechariah's hearing and speech. That evening, after putting John to bed, Elizabeth stepped outside and gazed up at the magnificent star-saturated sky.

---

[38] Luke 1:23

Overwhelmed, she fell to her knees. "Oh, Lord," she cried, tears of unimagined joy cascading down her face, "You have restored to me the hope I thought was dead. Oh, Lord, why would You bestow such goodness upon me in my older age? I am unworthy."

She had more to say but simply could not. However, in the deepest caverns of her soul, she heard her spirit speaking clearly. *Dear Lord, You are good, and in You is all hope. Sweet, wondrous hope!*

Elizabeth and You

Elizabeth had every reason to feel hopeless. She wanted children, but her body was incapable of producing them.

She knew and loved God, but perhaps she was not thinking of Him in the right terms, those that Isaiah expressed more than five centuries earlier: "It is I who made the earth and created mankind upon it. My own hands stretched out the heavens; I marshaled their starry hosts" (Isaiah 45:12). The aspect of God that Elizabeth did not consider was the God who creates *something* out of *nothing.*

Nothing ever existed on its own before God created it. It all came out of nothing!

If you are experiencing profound hopelessness, this truth should speak volumes to you. If you have lost your hope, then you can commiserate with Elizabeth, and even Job, who said, "What strength do I have, that I should still hope? What prospects, that I should be patient?" (Job 6:11).

If this is your question, then again hear Isaiah.

"See, I am doing a new thing! Now it springs up; do you not perceive it? I am making a way in the desert and streams in the wasteland" (Isaiah 43:19). Streams (plural!) in the wasteland? If the wasteland were full of streams, it would no longer be a wasteland.

And this is the point. You may think that your life is a desert, a wasteland. Whatever has happened to you has left you feeling empty and hopeless. You have prayed and strived, but nothing has worked. You may have even given up on God.

But don't surrender yet! And, whatever you do, don't obsess over your circumstances. Your vision is limited to what you can see. But God's isn't. God is not limited by circumstances as you are; in fact, He often considers them as nothing. This is because God is able to create new circumstances, circumstances that never existed and had no way of existing through human endeavor. God can—and does—create where nothing exists!

And this God who creates out of nothing has a message for you. He says: "For I am the Lord, your God, who takes hold of your right hand and says to you, Do not fear; I will help you" (Isaiah 41:13). Many well-wishers tell you to "hang in there," but they have no way to help you. God tells you to not fear, and He will help you. And yes, He has the ability to help you—even if this means creating a brand-new set of circumstances.

"See, I am doing a new thing!" Only God can say this and make it so. Because of God's creative prowess, you are *never* without hope! "But the needy will not always be forgotten, nor the hope of the afflicted ever perish" (Psalm 9:18).

The God who creates new things is the God who will never allow your hope to perish. He is the God of creation and hope, a dynamic combination that should fill your soul with assured expectation. Hope in the Lord—it will never be in vain!

Peter

Overcoming Failure

—«»→

As Peter sat waiting for a catch, he was oblivious to the other six disciples who shared the boat with him.

It was enough just to be sitting in the darkness of the Sea of Galilee, doing the thing he loved most in life. At least, what *used* to be the thing he loved most. Over the past three years, his love of fishing had been overtaken by his love for his Lord, Teacher, and Master, and in serving Him.

But now in the early morning stillness, Peter felt as if he had accomplished nothing over the previous three years. Suddenly, his self-inflicted brooding got the better of him. "This tongue of mine!" he startled the others with his unexpected outburst. "If only I can cut it out!"

Thomas was about to console him, but John stopped him with a nod. The others resumed their endeavors, acting as if the outburst never occurred. But it did occur, and it set off Peter's tortured mind, reigniting the revilement he had been pummeling himself with for the past two weeks.

Fool! he vilified himself, this time silently. *What a brave man you are! Hah! Did you really say, "Even if all fall away on account of you, I never will"? Fool! Bragger!* Peter spit in disgust. *And then,* he continued to denigrate himself, *you made even a bigger fool of yourself by proclaiming: "Even if I have to die with you, I will never disown you." Coward! Failure!*

Ah, that was it, Peter knew failure. His walk with Christ had been rife with it. Oh, sure, there were times of triumph, but they were always accompanied by dreadful failure—huge failure, overt failure, conspicuous failure, humiliating failure, detestable failure, spirit-crushing failure.

Yes, Peter's spirit was crushed. He had denied Christ—the one he so intrepidly vowed to die for—not once, not twice, but three times. "I don't know the man!" he bellowed that third time, spilling his wretched failure all over the courtyard of the high priest.

It was all too much for the Galilean to handle, but his mind was a whir of pain, confusion, and unceasing memories. And he could not turn it off. He remembered that he first met Jesus when his brother Andrew introduced him to the Rabbi from Nazareth. Peter had no idea what to think, especially when the Man with the burning eyes looked right at him and said, "You are Simon son of Jonah. From now on, you will be called Peter."

Before Peter could grasp the Rabbi's audacity, He stunned him yet again. "Come, follow me," He said, a gentle smile punctuating His words, "and I will make you fishers of men." Before Peter could fathom the command, he was following the Rabbi like a pet lamb.

Shortly after, Jesus wished to address the mobs that had come to hear Him speak. He asked Peter if He could use his boat as a platform, to which the fisherman gladly assented. When Jesus had finished speaking, He asked Peter to pull his boat out to the lake and let down his nets for a catch. Peter had spent the entire early morning fruitlessly seeking a haul and finally surrendered. Had anyone else made such an outrageous request, Peter would have either laughed him off or cursed him. But not so with the Rabbi. So, against his better judgment, Peter rowed out to sea.

Before he knew it, his nets were at the breaking point. Peter was overcome by the reality of the Rabbi's true identity. "Go away from me, Lord," he stammered, his body bent low at Jesus' feet, his face anchored to the floor of the boat. "I am a sinful man!"

Israel's long-awaited Messiah had come to him, and the fisherman feared him. From that time forward, Peter would experience momentous highs the likes of which he could never imagine. For instance, when many of Jesus' disciples turned away from Him, the Lord asked His twelve disciples, "You do not want to leave me too, do you?"

While the others hesitated, Peter knew what to say. "Lord, to whom shall we go? You have the words of eternal life. We have come to believe and to know that you are the Holy Christ of God." Jesus smiled and the fisherman was so proud.

But there was also the time when the disciples were in a boat in the middle of the lake and Jesus came walking out to them on the water. Stunned, Peter asked Jesus for the power to do the same.

The Lord granted it to him. But after a few steps, Peter realized the impossibility of what he was doing. He began to sink and begged Jesus to save him. "You of little faith," Jesus told him. "Why did you doubt?" At that moment, Peter wished that the Lord had allowed him to drown.

Then there was the time Jesus asked His disciples to tell Him who the people thought He was. "Some say John the Baptist, Elijah, or one of the prophets."

"But," Jesus countered, "who do you say I am?" As the others went mute, Peter knew exactly what to say. "You are the Messiah, the Son of the living God." Jesus embraced him and told him that upon that confession, He would build what He would soon call His Church. Peter was euphoric.

Then came that incredible Passover night, when Peter vowed his dying allegiance to Jesus. "I tell you the truth, Peter," Jesus said, tears rolling down His cheeks, "this very night, before the rooster crows, you will deny me three times."

"Never, Lord. Never!"

Hours later, consumed by smothering fear following the arrest of his Master, Peter did exactly what Jesus said he would do. And with it, he felt like walking death. He felt even worse following Jesus' crucifixion. He felt it even deeper at Jesus' resurrection. He felt more shamed than ever after Jesus' two appearances to the disciples.

And now, in the boat, he felt failure oozing out of every pore of his body. He did not even notice that it was now light until an intrusive voice interrupted his abusive meditations. "Friends, have you caught any fish?" a man on the shore called to them.

They answered negatively, much to Peter's exasperation, wishing his mates would ignore the stranger and send him on his way. However, the man persisted. "Throw your net on the right side of the boat and you will find some fish."

Peter rolled his eyes in disgust as the others obliged. "Right side?" he barked. "This is the most ridiculous thing I ever…" But before he knew it, the other six were struggling to heave in the teeming net. Peter felt a forceful smack on his back. "Peter!" John gushed, "It is the Lord!"

The truth struck the inconsolable fisherman like a lightning bolt. Before he knew it, he had hurled himself into the lake and began swimming toward shore. When he arrived, Jesus was there to take his hand. The Lord said nothing; He simply smiled with unworldly affection.

When the others arrived by boat, Jesus invited them to breakfast with Him. When they had finished eating, He turned to Peter. "Come, my friend, let us walk along the shore." Peter struggled to control the pounding of his racing heart. Jesus sensed this and walked slowly, giving Peter the opportunity to calm himself. When he did, Jesus put His arm around Peter's shoulder.

"Tell me, Simon son of Jonah, do you love me more than these others?"

"Yes, Lord," Peter struggled, hardly able to speak. "You know I love you."

"Feed my lambs."

They continued to walk in silence before Jesus stopped and faced Peter. "Simon son of Jonah, do you love me?"

Peter was confused but answered directly. "Yes, Lord," he repeated, "you know that I love you."

"Take care of my sheep."

They now turned and headed back to the others. "Simon son of Jonah," Jesus said again, this time not stopping, "do you love me?"

Peter felt like crying. How could Jesus keep asking the same question? On top of regarding Peter a failure, did Jesus also now think Peter was a liar? "Lord, you know all things; you know that I love you."

This time Jesus *did* stop and opened His arms wide. Peter fell into them and began to weep. When he was finished, Jesus released him. "Feed my sheep, Peter."

And with those words, the embattled failure of a disciple felt the wretchedness of his monstrous inadequacy peel away from him like a snake shedding its skin. He felt new and reborn, salvaged and reconstructed. And at that miraculous life-transforming moment, he knew one thing for certain: the colossal failure of a fisherman named Simon son of Jonah had died and was replaced by a man named Peter. A man deemed worthy to carry on the work of the Master.

Peter and You

Have you ever denied knowing the Lord as Peter did?

That's a loaded question, isn't it? For instance, were you ever in a discussion at work about God and when others spoke against Him, you were silent? It wasn't quite the same as denying Jesus the way Peter did, but your silence definitely did nothing to advance the cause of the Kingdom of God.

If you ever neglected to speak up for the Lord and was afterward convicted, then no doubt you felt the sting of failure. Of course, what made Peter's situation so much worse is that he boldly proclaimed that, "Even if I have to die with you, I will never disown you" (Matthew 26:35).

It is quite possible that you, too, have not kept your part of the bargain. Did you ever make a promise to Jesus, something like, "Lord, I promise to share the Gospel with twenty people this year," then neglect to do it? Or how about this one: "Lord, this is the year I'm going to discipline myself and read through all sixty-six books of the Bible." Yet, by the end of the year, you hadn't even made it halfway through. These are examples of spiritual failure.

An even worse instance of spiritual failure is the blatant sin against God's commands, such as sexual immorality, lying, stealing…well, you get it.

Though as a Christian you have been saved by the shed blood of Christ, always remember that the work of sanctification—God's molding of your character—is a lifetime work. Perfection will never be reached so long as you exist in the flesh; it can only come in eternity when God casts off your physical body and replaces it with a new, spiritual one (1 Corinthians 15:35–54).

"That's all well and good," you may be saying, "but what do I do now—in *this* lifetime—when I fail?" Great question.

First, a practical piece of advice: When the Jewish leaders brought to Jesus a woman caught in adultery, He told her, "Go now and leave your life of sin." In other words, "You failed once, don't do it again." Of course, not sinning is impossible, but what Jesus was getting at here was the willing, active *lifestyle* of sin. Look at the areas in your life that cause you to fail and ask God to give you the strength to stop.

Second, know your position as a Christian. The apostle Paul tells us that, "We are more than conquerors through him who loved us" (Romans 8:37). Being a conqueror is as far from failure as you can get! In fact, Paul also says that, "I can do everything through him who gives me strength" (Philippians 4:13).

Yes, like Peter, you will fail from time to time. EVERY Christian does. However, as God's elect, always remember that you are a conqueror who can do all things through the power of Christ.

Overcoming failure is one of them!

Matthew

Overcoming an Evil Past

←❮❯→

"And surely I am with you always, to the very end of the age."[39]

It was finished. He had done it. He had told the story of his Lord and Master, Jesus Christ. He had been at it for quite a time, but the work was finally over. "Thank you, Lord," he exulted, "for allowing Your servant to write Your story."

He decided to go out and get some air on the roof of his home. He had not gone outdoors much of late, so this time alone under the deep blue sky was a rare pleasure. He was delighted yet restrained, exhilarated yet reflective. This was the crowning achievement of his life, and yet he could not help thinking back to how he had gotten here.

Now in his mid-sixties, the white-haired author emitted a laugh. "The Gospel of our Lord ... by a filthy tax collector. Oh, Lord, please bless this work."

---

[39] Matthew 28:20

Matthew knew something about blessings. Growing up under his given name of Levi, he and his family lived in a remote area of the Galilee. His father Alphaeus was a farmer, one who toiled endlessly in the fields in the burning heat from sunup to sundown, supporting a family of five in their modest home.

Levi's early years were good ones. As a typical Hebrew-Aramaic-speaking boy, he began school at age five, sitting with the other kids at the feet of the village rabbi and learning how to read and write Hebrew. The bulk of the study, however, centered on the sacred scriptures, and Levi absolutely loved his education.

But he also loved something else. During his family's annual trips to Capernaum and the lake of Galilee, Levi would note some of the larger homes in the city, several of which were four and five times more substantial than his own. He also noticed that the people coming from them were dressed in rich, ornate clothing of exotic fabrics from other lands, with their fingers and necks arrayed in glittering, gaudy jewelry. Levi had never seen anything like them.

"Come, Levi!" Alphaeus would bark whenever he noticed his impressionable son gazing in awe at the affluent.

By age ten, Levi wanted to know why his father was always steering him away from the sight of these well-garbed men. "These pigs are tax collectors, Levi," Alphaeus would spit with disdain. "They are the worst kind of people. Avoid them whenever you can."

"Why is this, Father?"

"Because they are traitors to our people. They are Hebrews, as we are, but work for Rome. They collect taxes for Rome and rob their own people, us—in the process. They are worse than lepers."

Levi had once seen a leper, and it was disturbing. "Why are they worse than lepers?"

"At least," Alphaeus explained, "lepers do not choose to be lepers. But these leeches..."

He was too disgusted to finish. Despite his father's contempt of this substratum of Jewish society, Levi could not help but be drawn to them. By age thirteen, he had grown tall, and Alphaeus needed him in the fields. The young teen was crushed. He loved attending school, his education a satisfying cerebral challenge to his growing intellect. Now that was over.

For the next five years, he worked in the fields—and hated every moment of it. He saw what it had done to his father. Alphaeus was hunched over, his skin dried out like withered papyrus, and he barely made enough of a living to keep the family fed.

By age eighteen, Levi announced that he was leaving home and moving to Capernaum. "Stay away from the tax collectors!" Alphaeus warned.

Levi headed straight toward them. He began his tax-collecting career as a *gabbai*, one who collected general taxes on land, property, and income. However, after two years of earning a meager existence, he realized that a more affluent lifestyle lay in being a *mokhe*. As a *mokhe*, Levi collected a wide variety of taxes, including import fees, business license fees, and toll fees.

For tax collectors, life was best in Capernaum, a customs post on the caravan route from Damascus to the Mediterranean Sea. By the time he was twenty-four, Levi had his own booth on the major international road. By the time he was twenty-eight, he had become a wealthy man.

He paid a heavy price for it. He had come to learn that a tax collector's wealth was not derived *merely* from collecting taxes. It came through extortion. Tax collectors became rich through extracting as much money from their fellow Jews as possible above the required Roman tax rate. They were allowed to go as high as they could so long as their corruption did not lead to revolt.

Levi became adept at knowing just how high he could go with each hapless citizen he gouged. He also learned what it was to be hated and ostracized by the Jewish community. As a tax collector, Levi was banned from the great synagogue of Capernaum—the religious and civic nucleus of town life. He was lumped together socially with the worst of the town's sinners—adulterers, thieves, prostitutes, and moneylenders.

By age thirty, he had achieved his every goal—and was miserable. He had not spoken to his family for years, they having banished him long ago. He missed them terribly and buried his sorrow in wild parties, wine, and perverted practices. He had come to hate his life.

Then one day, Levi noticed a stir. Upon investigation, he discovered that a Rabbi from Nazareth had roused the people with his teaching about love and faith. Levi decided to investigate.

Disguising himself, he took his place among a mountainside throng gathered around the Rabbi.

"Blessed are the poor in spirit, for theirs is the kingdom of heaven," the Rabbi taught. "Blessed are those who mourn, for they will be comforted. Blessed are the meek, for they will inherit the earth. Blessed are those who hunger and thirst for righteousness, for they will be filled."[40]

The Rabbi's words radiated through Levi's aching soul and brought tender healing. The Rabbi's voice permeated the tax collector's icy heart, melting the frigidness that had encrusted it.

Life in his tax booth became unbearable. He loathed what he did for a living and hated everything about his life. He decided to try honesty—collecting *only* the taxes that Rome required without taking anymore for himself. Every opportunity he got, he went to listen to the Rabbi. And whenever he did, his soul was shattered all over again.

And then, on one unusual day, as he sat in his booth, the Rabbi and his men passed by. Levi's heart began to pound as never before. It thundered even more violently when the Rabbi stopped and looked at him. Levi felt as if he would collapse. Then the Rabbi spoke. "Follow me." It was all he needed to hear. Levi's tax-collecting days were over. A few hours later, he summoned the courage to approach the Rabbi.

---

[40] Matthew 5:3–6

"Lord," he said kneeling, "would you do me the honor of coming to my house tonight for a banquet in your honor?"

"Name the time, Levi."

The new disciple cried for the first time in his adult life.

The next two-and-one-half years were the most extraordinary of Levi's life. For one thing, he had been given a new name, Matthew—"gift of God." For another, he was able to invest his life in that of the Rabbi's and receive an education he never could have imagined when he was a boy learning in the synagogue. He began to write down accounts of Jesus' life as they happened, focusing on his teachings and sermons. They were extraordinary times indeed, even the last days, which culminated with Jesus's crucifixion.

Which was no culmination at all. When Jesus appeared to Matthew and his fellow disciples following His resurrection, Matthew's spirits was raised as well, and he knew he would spend the rest of his life spreading the good news of his Lord and Savior. By the time he reached his sixties and realized that his years were becoming few, he knew he had to give the world the story of all he had witnessed, learned, and come to accept as truth: that Jesus Christ was the only way to salvation and everlasting life.

With the guidance of the Holy Spirit, he sat down one day and began to write: "A record of the genealogy of Jesus Christ the son of David, the son of Abraham."[41] And now it was finished.

---

[41] Matthew 1:1

The final words had been penned.

As he sat back looking into the blue sky, he still could not conceal his amazement.

"Are you sure about this, Lord?" he mused. "The story of Your Son, as told by a filthy tax collector?"

He then released a joyous laugh, knowing that Jesus would not have wanted it any other way.

Matthew and You

For the most part, tax collectors were vile and evil men.

The act of tax collecting was not in itself evil—it was the extortion of hardworking men and women that made it so. Matthew profited handsomely from this repulsive practice, and he was deservedly regarded as an evil man. Until, that is, Jesus got a hold of him.

What about you? Have you at one time been involved in evil practices? Drug dealing? Vandalism? Violence? Do you, even now, still practice certain behavior you know you shouldn't?

What does the Bible say about this? A great place to start is the book of Isaiah. There, the prophet tells Israel—and you: "Let the wicked forsake his way and the evil man his thoughts. Let him turn to the Lord, and he will have mercy on him, and to our God, for he will freely pardon" (Isaiah 55:7). If you have lived an evil life, then this should be your life verse. Though just a few words, it's loaded with meaning!

First, notice the act of will that is being encouraged here. Telling the wicked to "forsake" his way is like saying, "Stop doing what you are doing!" That's about as direct as it gets. The message to you is the same. If you know Christ as your Lord and Savior, no doubt you have *pretty much* halted your former practices—but perhaps not completely. If this is the case, then Isaiah is telling you to "stop it this instant!"

Second, notice the command to forsake your "evil thoughts." It is possible that you no longer *act* the way you once did, but perhaps you still *think* about what you once did. The thought life is a dangerous thing as it eventually leads to practice. James, the apostle, explains it well: "When tempted, no one should say, 'God is tempting me.' For God cannot be tempted by evil, nor does he tempt anyone; but each one is tempted when, by his own evil desire, he is dragged away and enticed. Then, after desire has conceived, it gives birth to sin; and sin, when it is full-grown, gives birth to death" (James 1:13–15).

The message is clear. If you have lived an evil life and now belong to Christ, you have been set free. However, if remnants of that evil still linger in practice and thought, put an immediate end to it. That's the practical side.

Now the reassuring side. The Isaiah verse closes by saying, "Turn to the Lord, and he will have mercy on [you], and to our God, for he will freely pardon." Accepting Jesus Christ is to accept mercy for your sins, redemption from your evil ways, and reward of eternal life. You have gone from condemned sinner to righteous child of

God. The evilness of your flesh is dead and buried as you walk a new life of faith and serving Him.

If Levi the evil tax collector could become a new creature in Christ, then so can you!

Thomas

OVERCOMING DOUBT

―❮❯―

What madness is this? Thomas agonized as he wandered the empty streets of Jerusalem near midnight.

They have seen the Lord? Impossible! It cannot be! They are delusional. He wanted to believe it.

He really did. But his skepticism would not permit it. His pessimism would not afford him this luxury of pure faith. His inherent doubt would wage war against his deepest desire. *How can I believe it? How can they believe it? All ten of them! It defies all logic!*

And yet that was what his fellow disciples had sworn to him. "We have seen the Lord!" they proclaimed as one. They said it again and again, trying to breach through Thomas's defiant doubt.

If only I were there!

But Thomas was not there on that Sunday night following Jesus' crucifixion three days earlier. That was the night the disciples claimed that Jesus appeared to them. Though the room they met in was locked from fear of the Jewish authorities, Jesus was with them. The disciples said they were sitting around contemplating their future when, in an instant, Jesus was among them.

"It is the truth," Peter assured Thomas the next day when the grieving disciple returned to them. He had been roaming the streets of the city trying to make sense of all that had occurred.

"Jesus said, 'Peace be with you,'" Peter told him.

Thomas could not believe it then, and he could not believe it now. But Peter was not done. "He showed us His wrists that had been pierced by the nails and His side where the Roman soldier had thrust his sword. The wounds were still there."

Thomas could only stand mute in mesmerized disbelief. Seeing that Peter was not getting through to Thomas, John—Jesus' most beloved of all the disciples—came to his aid. "What Peter says is accurate, Thomas," he implored. "He spoke to us about many things, and before He left, the Master said, 'As the Father has sent me, I am sending you. Receive the Holy Spirit. If you forgive anyone his sins, they are forgiven; if you do not forgive them, they are not forgiven.' It happened exactly that way, Thomas."

The rest chorused their assent, but Thomas, heart shattered, could not accept it. He took firm hold of Peter's shoulders and voiced his objection. "Unless I see the nail marks in His wrists and put my finger where the nails were, and put my hand into His side, I will not believe it."

Peter began to reason with him again, but John stopped him. "He must see for himself, Peter. This is between Thomas and the Master."

And now, one week later, Thomas was as miserable as ever. *Oh, Lord,* he cried out from the caverns of his soul, *why did you ever leave us? Why!* Yet Thomas well knew that this was exactly what Jesus said

He would do. In fact, He had spent the last half of His three years of ministry preparing them for His inevitable departure. But they did not understand. They did not *want* to understand.

"Do not let your hearts be troubled," Jesus had encouraged His men several days before His death. "Trust in God; trust also in me." *Do not let your hearts be troubled?* Thomas silently questioned incredulously. *You have been preaching to us about your death. How can we not have troubled hearts?*

The Master's death—this was Thomas's greatest fear. He had been called by Jesus to become one of His followers. That Thomas so readily agreed was unlike anything he had ever done. It usually took Thomas weeks to decide crucial matters, so when Jesus asked him to leave his family and become one of His disciples, Thomas's instant acceptance was astonishing. But Thomas knew there was something different about this Rabbi from Nazareth. Of course, there were the miracles. Though they impressed practically everyone else, they were not what made Thomas's heart pulsate. What ignited Thomas's soul were the Master's teachings. *Oh, the depth of His words!* Thomas would find his spirit rejoicing. *How can a man speak such glorious words?*

But that was just it. Though Jesus *was* a man, He was so much more than that. He was sent from God Himself. In fact, he had even proclaimed that He and God were one.[42] Thomas was not quite sure what that meant, only that Jesus was no *ordinary* man. He had also claimed to be the Messiah of Israel, and Thomas believed it.

---

[42] John 10:30

But the claims of deity...and His pending death...and the urging to not be discouraged...

"In my Father's house are many rooms," Jesus continued speaking that night. "I am going there to prepare a place for you. And if I go and prepare a place for you, I will come back and take you to be with me that you also may be where I am. You know the way to the place where I am going."

The disciples looked at each other and had no idea what Jesus was talking about other than He was leaving them to go somewhere—apparently for their benefit—and that He would return to take them with Him. Thomas did not like the fact that Jesus would be leaving him. He also abhorred the fact that no one had the guts to ask Jesus to explain Himself.

Except him. "Lord," he said, "we do not know where you are going, so how can we know the way?"

Jesus looked at Thomas and smiled. The disciple's heart melted. "I am the way and the truth and the life," he said lovingly, firmly, confidently. "No one comes to the Father except through Me. If you really knew Me, you would know my Father as well. From now on, you do know Him and have seen Him."

Thomas still did not understand. He was too disturbed. He had wanted Jesus to tell him that He would *not* be leaving them, but instead Jesus had met Thomas's pain with a point of incomprehensible theology. But now, one week following Jesus' alleged visit to the disciples, it suddenly began making sense. Thomas mulled Jesus' words as he turned and began heading back to the disciples' quarters.

Jesus consistently referred to God as His "Father." He claimed that if people knew Him, then they would also know *His* Father. Jesus. The Father. They were one, Jesus said. They were one.

Thomas could not walk quickly enough, so he began jogging to return to his companions. He felt something spurring him on, a strange hope that was foreign to him. When he reached the disciples' quarters just past midnight, he knocked. When Peter opened the door for him, Thomas was relieved to see the torches lit and the ten still awake. "We have been praying for you, Thomas," Peter told him. "We are so glad to see you. Come, have a drink."

As Peter bolted the door, Thomas made His way to the other end of the room. Suddenly, a voice shattered the stillness. "Peace be with you!"

Thomas looked...and turned white. It was the Master. He felt as if His heart would come crashing through his chest. It began to pump even more furiously when Jesus looked directly at him. "Thomas, dear Thomas," the Master gently said, walking toward him. "Put your finger here; see My wrists. Reach out your hand and put it into My side. Stop doubting and believe."

But Thomas would not look at the scars. He saw nothing but Jesus' eyes as they exuded love, mercy, tenderness, gentleness, and most of all, compassion. Thomas's legs began to buckle and grow weak. They could no longer carry the weight of his trembling body.

He fell to his knees, his eyes beginning to well up. He never once took his gaze off the Master. He had no intention of touching Jesus' wrists or side. There was no need to. And from the depths of his soul—places he did not even know existed—he found himself proclaiming the words he had finally come to understand as truth. The only truth.

"My Lord and my God!"

There was no longer any doubt in Thomas's mind. Jesus had shown Himself to him. He had come from—where did He come from?—just to make Himself known to Thomas. *Yes,* Thomas at last knew—*the Master is God. He has risen from the dead as He said He would.*

He is God! He is God! I will never doubt Him again!

Jesus had much to say that early morning to the disciples, but Thomas had difficulty concentrating. In fact, he never got off his knees the entire time Jesus was there, nor did he care to. Jesus had come to him and banished all doubt.

As Jesus spoke to the others, Thomas could but look upon Him, all along allowing his heart to express the glorious words:

My Lord and my God! My Lord and my God!

Thomas and You

Though a doubter, Thomas was also one of Jesus' most loyal followers, willing to die for Him if necessary (John 11:16).

He was also a natural skeptic and pessimist. There is nothing wrong with this. Such people—and perhaps you are one of them—must have proof. They are slow to accept, always needing to weigh everything before making a decision. This is commendable. Though doubt was a part of Thomas's nature, Jesus still told him, "Stop doubting and believe" (John 20:27). Was Jesus being too hard on Thomas?

What about you? Do you attend church, see others rejoicing in worship, and nodding affirmatively during the pastor's message but cannot join them because you question *everything?* Do you sometimes feel as if Jesus is saying to you, "Stop doubting and believe"?

If so, is He being too hard on you? He isn't.

Consider Thomas's error. It was not that he was a skeptic. If you, too, are a skeptic, you are to be commended. However, consider Thomas's words. When the other disciples told him about Jesus' first appearance to them, Thomas said, "Unless I see the nail marks in his hands and put my finger where the nails were, and put my hand into his side, *I will not believe it*" (John 20:25, *italics added*).

Though Thomas's sentiments were sincere, he stated boldly that he *refused* to believe anything he couldn't see for himself. Are you the same way? If so, you may require some spiritual tweaking.

In the book of Hebrews, the author says, "Faith is being sure of what we hope for and certain of what we do not see" (Hebrews 11:1). Though this may go against your inclination to doubt, true faith in Jesus requires this act of willing obedience. This may seem foolish to you, but the key is to think in spiritual terms, not human ones. The apostle Paul confirms this when he writes, "This is what we speak, not in words taught us by human wisdom but in words taught by the Spirit, expressing spiritual truths in spiritual words. The man without the Spirit does not accept the things that come from the Spirit of God, for they are foolishness to him, and he cannot understand them, because they are spiritually discerned" (1 Corinthians 2:13–14).

Where Thomas strayed, and perhaps you, is when he allowed foolish human thinking to hijack what the Spirit was telling him. Do you do the same thing? If you have accepted Jesus as your Lord and Savior, then you have the Holy Spirit dwelling within you (Ephesians 2:22). It is He—the Spirit—who "guide[s] you into all truth" (John 16:13). This guiding of the Spirit negates all doubt.

So, are you a little *too* similar to Thomas for comfort? Then let the Spirit help overcome your doubt and triumph over your pessimism. When you do, it will become a much easier matter to "stop doubting and believe."

Woman at the Well

OVERCOMING IMMORALITY

←❝❞→

Sheerah[43] felt the isolation.

The streets were full this early evening, but she knew she was alone. As she carried her pitcher through the town of Sychar in Samaria, she met with the usual downturned heads or gazes that looked beyond her to some distant sight. She hated that her home was so far from the town well and wished she lived much closer. Not only would it save her some exertion on her aging body, but it would spare her from her daily portion of village hostility.

Sheerah had been married five times—inexcusable by Hebrew standards and extreme even by those of Samaria. And now, the man she was living with was not her husband; he did not want to be number six in her growing collection of former spouses.

So, as Sheerah trekked to the Sychar well, she had to endure another torturous number of people acting as if they did not see her or cross to the other side of the street so they would not have to speak or greet her. She was used to it after all these years, but it never

---

[43] Character not named in the Bible. Name added to enrich story.

became easier. For every time she embarked upon her water-fetching duties, she felt as if her long years of immorality were on full display.

As she approached the well, like she did every day at this time, about six in the evening, she was glad to find the area empty—except for the odd sight of a lone man sitting just a few body lengths from the well. It was rare to find a man there, since drawing water was the domain of female servants and poorer women. But his presence was just a small part of Sheerah's confusion. As she drew nearer, she could tell by the way he was dressed and his facial features that this man was Jewish. *A Jew in Samaria,* she mused. *He must be lost.*

Even more puzzling to Sheerah was that this man was looking directly at her, which Jewish men hardly ever did to Jewish women, let alone Samaritans. *This is strange indeed,* Sheerah thought.

As she reached the well, the man smiled at her, a gesture she returned. She was about to lower her pitcher into the well when the man stunned her by speaking. "Excuse me," he said kindly, "will you mind giving me a drink of water?"

Sheerah looked up. "You are a Jew and I am a Samaritan. How can you ask me for a drink?" she asked stupefied. "The few Jewish men I have run across would just as soon spit at me than seek anything from my hand."

"Dear woman, if you only knew the gift of God and who it is that asks you for a drink, you would have asked him, and he would have given you living water."

Sheerah pondered his words. "*You* will give *me* a drink?" she asked, mystified. "But the well is deep, and you have nothing to draw water with. With what can you give me water? Are you greater than our father Jacob who drank from this very well?"

Sheerah was amazed that she was even having this conversation.

"Look down into the well," the man told her. She did. "Now, see the water," he continued. "Everyone who drinks this water will be thirsty again, but whoever drinks the water I give him will never thirst. The water I give will become in him a spring of water welling up to eternal life."

Never thirst again? Spring of water? Eternal life? Who is this man and what are these mysterious things of which he speaks?

"I am not sure what this water is you refer to," she said awkwardly, "but, sir, if you can give me some of this water, I would be grateful. This way I will not be thirsty and have to keep coming to this well day after day."

She thought the man would produce this water for her, but instead he just looked at her for several seconds, as if examining her. "Woman," he said in a tone more serious, "go home, call your husband, and come back."

She looked at him and wondered why he would make such a request. An invasive request at that. "I have no husband, sir."

The man smiled softly. "You are indeed right, dear woman, when you say you have no husband. In fact, you have had five husbands during your lifetime, and the man you now live with is not your husband. You do indeed speak the truth."

Sheerah began to tremble. She felt as if she had been stripped naked, her sin open and exposed. "Sir," she said, her voice quivering, "I can see that you are a prophet…"

She was terribly shaken. Who *was* this man who had claimed such full knowledge of her? Very few people in Sychar knew of her marital difficulties, let alone this Jew she had never seen before. She felt dark and dirty as she stood before him and did not wish to discuss the issue further.

She desperately tried changing the subject. "Sir," she said, "our fathers worshiped on this mountain, Gerizim, but you Jews claim that the place where we must worship is in Jerusalem. Which is correct?"

The man crossed his legs, his ease bringing Sheerah a degree of solace. "Believe me, woman, a time is coming when you will worship the Father neither on this mountain nor in Jerusalem."

Sheerah could not believe that this holy man would engage her in theological discourse. "You Samaritans," he continued, "worship what you do not know; we worship what we do know, for salvation is from the Jews. Yet a time is coming—and has now come—when the true worshipers will worship the Father in spirit and truth, for they are the kind of worshipers the Father seeks. God is spirit, and his worshipers must worship in spirit and in truth."

It was too much for Sheerah to comprehend, but she was struck by the depth, the conviction, the… absolute truth of his extraordinary words. This was like no man she had ever met.

"I know that Messiah is coming," she replied, not knowing what else to say. "When he comes, he will explain everything to us."

The man then rose and looked solemnly at her. "I who speak to you am he."

Sheerah dropped her pitcher and looked at him. She felt her knees go weak and began trembling once again. She did not know if she should bow to him or…

Suddenly, she heard a small clamor a short distance off. A group of about ten or eleven men was approaching. They came directly to the man, and Sheerah could tell that he was their leader.

She was convinced. Leaving her pitcher, she turned quickly and began running to the heart of the village. As people saw her coming, they began to scatter, hoping to avoid her. She spotted a group of men and ran straight toward them. They viewed her with appalled confusion and degrading disgust.

She ignored their insulting glares. "Gentlemen," she gushed, looking from one to another. "You must come with me. I have just spoken with a man who told me everything I ever did."

They looked at her as if she were deranged. "I speak the truth to you," she insisted more desperately. "This man is like no one you have ever met. Can he be the Christ? Can he be the one we are waiting for?"

The men looked at each other in wonder, then back at her. "What madness is this you speak of, woman?" one of the village leaders questioned. "You have seen the Christ? And he has spoken to you and not to us?"

"I cannot explain why he appeared to me, but please come. See for yourselves. He is now at the well. You can ask him anything you want. Why would I make something like this up?"

The men thought for a moment. "Take us to him, woman."

For the next three hours, the men of Samaria sat at Jesus' feet and listened to every word He said. In fact, He remained two more days with them, and many became His followers.

As Jesus dismissed them on His final day with them, a group of men approached Sheerah. "Now we have heard for ourselves, woman. We know that this Man really is the Savior of the world. We thank you for bringing us to Him."

As the others walked away, Sheerah found a large rock and sat on it. *The Savior of the world. And He came to me. Oh why, Lord? Why would You show Yourself to me? A sinner, a vile sinner. An immoral and ignorant woman.*

And then she understood. She was no longer any of these things. The Savior had cleansed her. Her days of immorality were over. She belonged to the Savior and would be forever clean!

She then slowly approached the well and looked down. *Living water. Yes, Lord, you are my eternal spring of living water!*

Woman at the Well and You

The woman at the well lived a sinful life. Five husbands and living with a man who was not her husband? By biblical standards, she was beyond doubt an immoral woman.

What about you? Did you live an immoral life? Since coming to Christ, have you ceased your immoral ways but still have trouble overcoming the guilt? If so, you must learn to bury those days for good.

First, consider that Jesus came to earth to die for people exactly like you. When Jesus was discovered attending a party thrown by hated tax collectors, the Pharisees asked Jesus' disciples, "Why does your teacher eat with tax collectors and 'sinners'?" (Matthew 9:11).

Jesus replied, "It is not the healthy who need a doctor, but the sick. But go and learn what this means: 'I desire mercy, not sacrifice.' For I have not come to call the righteous, but sinners" (Matthew 9:12–13).

There is no one whom Jesus considers unworthy of salvation. You no doubt understand this, but still you wonder. Perhaps you were molested by a relative and are still reliving the shame of it. Perhaps you were sexually active and still feel humiliated by your actions. Maybe you engaged in illegal activity and still can't forgive yourself.

If you suffer from the inability to overcome your past immorality, the Bible has some encouragement for you. The apostle Paul writes, "Do you not know that the wicked will not inherit the kingdom of God? Do not be deceived: Neither the sexually immoral nor idolaters nor adulterers nor male prostitutes nor homosexual offenders nor thieves nor the greedy nor drunkards nor slanderers nor swindlers will inherit the kingdom of God. And that is what some of you were. But you were washed, you were sanctified, you were justified in the name of the Lord Jesus Christ and by the Spirit of our God" (1 Corinthians 6:9–11).

The first part of the verse is rather sorted: sexually immoral, adulterers, thieves, drunkards. Not exactly an upstanding crowd of people. And yet all these men and women were—*and are*—part of the Church of Jesus Christ. Notice how Paul says, "And that's what some of you *were*." In other words, their past actions did not keep them from being Christ's followers. But note the second part of the verse: "…you were washed…sanctified…justified…in the name of the Lord Jesus Christ…"

This is the answer to your past sin and the guilt you still carry from it. It's time to stop carrying it! Instead, right now, say out loud: "In the name of the Lord Jesus Christ, I am washed! I am sanctified! I am justified!"

This is not some empty mantra or hollow formula, but God-breathed, soul-invigorating, truth-empowered words of fact, salvation, and restoration. And if you know Jesus Christ as your Lord and Savior, this is *your* truth as well.

Washed. Sanctified. Justified. This is who and what you are! Now!

So, what's all this to do about your past immorality? It's dead and buried—let it go once and for all!

Martha

Overcoming Disappointment

←«»→

"**H**ow can Mary just sit there while I do all the work!" Martha said just loud enough only for her to hear. "Does she know how many people are here?"

Martha was right—there were many people in her spacious home in Bethany, just two miles east of Jerusalem. The reason for the insurgence of guests was the presence of Jesus, the Rabbi from Nazareth, whom Martha, her sister Mary, and brother Lazarus had befriended about a year ago. They had opened their home to him whenever He visited Jerusalem, and today was one of those times.

As Jesus taught, He was surrounded by his twelve disciples, the women who traveled with them, and Martha's many neighbors. There was food to be served, feet to be washed, and cups of wine and water to be poured. Martha could always rely on Mary to help her entertain guests, but today she was acting like one of them! As Martha hustled through her chores, she could not help but cast resentful looks at Mary, who sat mesmerized at the Rabbi's feet.

How can she be so heartless! Martha fumed. Martha, the matriarch of the house, understood that her younger sister was more of the emotional one while she was the practical one. But Mary was always there for her when needed. However, this present lack of allegiance was, to Martha's way of thinking, difficult to accept. Finally, when she could no longer hold her peace, Martha put down the tray she was carrying and navigated her way through the crowd to where Jesus was sitting. Because Martha was the only one standing, she was impossible to ignore.

Jesus stopped speaking and looked up at her, His eyes inviting her to say what was on her mind. "Lord, do You not care that my sister has left me to do the work by myself? Tell her to help me!"[44] she ventured, the annoyance evident in her tone,

It seemed like a reasonable request to Martha. After all, the Rabbi knew all about propriety and organization. Not too long ago, He was so angered by the corruption in the temple court that He cleared it of all moneychangers and animal merchants.[45] If anyone would be sympathetic to her, it would be Jesus. She felt even more confident of His support when He smiled.

"Martha, Martha," He said, love pouring from His lips like a waterfall. "You are worried and upset about many things, but only

---

[44] Luke 10:40

[45] The Bible records two separate times when Jesus "cleared" the temple. John 2:17–22 tells of an incident early in His ministry, and Mark 11:12–19 tells of the other near the end of His ministry.

one thing is needed. Mary has chosen what is better, and it will not be taken away from her."[46]

Stunned, Martha felt defeated, deflated, disappointed. She had been working furiously to make the Rabbi's visit a comfortable experience for both He and her guests. Mary, on the other hand, was doing nothing but sitting and listening. *Surely, Rabbi,* she cried within, *You cannot be so indifferent to my plight.* She stood looking at Him for an awkward moment feeling empty and betrayed. She wanted to voice her defiance, her dismay, but was too hurt. She gazed deeply into Jesus' eyes, looking for some shred of consolation. He continued to smile tenderly at her, like her father did when he chastised her as a girl. It was a smile that said, "Oh, Martha, you know how much I love you and always will, but at this moment, you are wrong."

Not wishing to make any more of a spectacle of herself than she already has, she slowly turned, head down, and returned to the kitchen. When she arrived, she began to load up a platter with cheeses and fruits, but she lost heart and put it back down. "Oh, Lord," she said quietly, "did You have to give me such a response. Do You know how much I love You? If not, would I have opened my home to You as I have? And, dearest Jesus, how could You have praised Mary for simply sitting at your feet while I have toiled without rest? Oh, Lord, I am stung by disappointment."

---

[46] Luke 10:41–42

Over the following weeks, Martha would often replay the incident, trying to make sense of the Rabbi's words. *Why would He compliment Mary but reprove me? What great thing did she do that I didn't?* And then, after about a month of such self-punishment, God gave her peace. Jesus *did* appreciate everything she did and loved her deeply, but He wanted more of her. He wanted her heart, her soul, her deepest love, her very life.

As Martha asked God for forgiveness and for the ability to love her Lord in a deeper way, she felt her faith begin to strengthen, her devotion begin to grow. And how desperately she would need that faith and devotion! A year later, Lazarus had gotten sick, very sick. Deathly sick. Martha sent a pressing message to Jesus telling Him about her brother's condition and pleading with Him to come quickly.

But Jesus did not come quickly. As the two sisters fervently prayed, Lazarus's condition grew gravely worse. Finally, he died. Fiercely disappointed that Jesus did not come to Lazarus's rescue, Martha made the arrangements to have Lazarus buried in a cave with a stone laid across the entrance. Four days later, word reached Martha that Jesus had arrived with His contingent and was just outside the city. "Come, Mary," Martha said, "let us go to Him."

Mary, however, was too overcome with grief to make the short trek, so Martha went by herself. When she reached Jesus, she fell to her feet, rose, and allowed Him to embrace her. "Lord," she said, stepping back, "if You had been here, my brother would not have died. But I know that even now God will give You whatever you ask."

She simply meant that she trusted that Jesus somehow could turn this tragic situation into a blessing. He smiled tenderly at her. "Martha, your brother will rise again."

She believed in the resurrection at the end of the age and expressed her agreement that, yes, her brother *would* one day be resurrected. At this, Jesus' eyes widened, demanding Martha's absolute attention. "I am the resurrection and the life," He said. "He who believes in Me will live, even though he dies; and whoever lives and believes in Me will never die. Do you believe this?"[47]

The meaning was obscure to Martha, but she *did* understand that Jesus had been expressing to her something of extreme importance. She felt His very words pierce through her heart and bury themselves deeply within her soul. She shuddered at the essence of who this Man of God—this God—was.

"Yes, Lord," she found herself saying, "I believe that you are the Christ, the Son of God, who was to come into the world."[48]

And with this incredible confession, Jesus once again smiled, as if commending Martha for a job well done. She felt the joy and contentment of His approval, the pleasure and gratification of His reassurance. It was as if He had said to her, *I am so proud of you, my beloved daughter!* At Jesus' urging, Martha, her strength renewed,

---

[47] John 11:25–26
[48] John 11:27

returned home and accompanied Mary to the Rabbi. Once comforting Mary, Jesus asked Martha to take Him to the tomb.

At their arrival, Jesus ordered the stone at the cave's entrance to be rolled away. But always the practical one, Martha objected. "Lord, by this time there is a bad odor, for he has been there four days."

Again, Jesus looked at her and smiled reassuringly. "Dear Martha"—His words were like healing balm to her aching heart—"did I not tell you that if you believed, you would see the glory of God?"[49]

Martha felt a surge of joy and expectation flooding her consciousness. Jesus prayed, then looked up. Martha's heart began to race.

"Lazarus," Jesus commanded, "come out!"

Martha stood transfixed by what was occurring. And then she saw the impossible. Still wrapped head to toe in his burial clothes, Lazarus appeared. Martha fell to her knees in incomprehensible joy and fear. And in her euphoria, she looked up at Jesus. Sensing this, the Lord looked down at her, smiled, and offered His hand to help her to her feet.

However, before accepting His offer, Martha hesitated. She was exactly where she needed to be—at Jesus' feet. The distress of past disappointment had been wonderfully lifted and obliterated. Like her sister had done a year ago, so Martha now gloried at Jesus' feet.

---

[49] John 11:40

Yes, there would soon be much to do, and she would have to see that it got done. But for now, Martha was content to worship at her Lord's feet.

She was in no hurry to rise.

Martha and You

Martha's disappointment was profound. She worked furiously to make Jesus' visit as comfortable for both He and her guests as possible.

And yet Jesus told her that her sister Mary, who "only" sat at Jesus' feet and listened, did better than she. This was difficult for Martha to hear—and so disappointing!

What about you? Are you disappointed? Have you put your faith in Jesus, worked hard to serve Him but don't feel appreciated, or you sense that your work for Him is in vain? Such thoughts are common when you lose the focus of your service—Jesus. Yes, your good works are for the benefit of people, but your motivation comes from a desire to serve God.

This is the key to overcoming and triumphing over any disappointment that comes your way. Strive to know Jesus on a far deeper level. Make this the absolute goal of your life, and disappointment will disappear.

The apostle Paul was consumed with getting to know Jesus as deeply and as humanly possible. He wrote, "I want to know Christ and the power of his resurrection and the fellowship of sharing in his sufferings, becoming like him in his death, and so, somehow, to attain to the resurrection from the dead" (Philippians 3:9–10). This is radical and life-transforming stuff! Paul is expressing an almost transcendent desire to know Christ, one that defies normal human comprehension.

This is where Martha fell short, but where Mary got it right. Yes, Martha most certainly loved Jesus and worked diligently to serve Him, but most of what she did was on the exterior—the work of the flesh. Mary, on the other hand, sought to know Jesus on a deeper level. She sat at His feet as He spoke. He had come to Martha's house to share vital truths about Himself, eternal life, and redemption. It was more important that His words be heard than His audience be served.

If you have been disappointed despite your good works for Christ, take your eyes off people and put all of your hope in Christ. He is the One who can uplift you and give you a sense of worth and expectation. Paul writes, "Hope does not disappoint us, because God has poured out his love into our hearts by the Holy Spirit, whom he has given us" (Romans 5:5).

Hope is the opposite of disappointment, but hope centered on Jesus—not people. People will more often than not disappoint you, as you more often than you care to admit disappoint others. But in the desire to know Christ more richly and deeply and to follow Him more closely and intimately, you will transform your disappointment into hope.

In time, Martha was able to confidently assert to Jesus, "I believe that you are the Christ, the Son of God, who was to come into the world" (John 11:27). What do you say about Jesus and how do you view Him?

The answer is often the difference between discouraging disappointment and blessed hope!

The Woman Who Washed Jesus' Feet

OVERCOMING SHAME

Sinner!

The name washed over her like a wave in a thunderstorm, assuring her condemnation, deepening her shame.

Sinner!

The word hounded her every step, proclaiming her guilt, dooming her soul. Of course, Neriah[50] knew that the people of the Galilean village of Nain who labeled her with the hateful epithet were absolutely right. She was a prostitute—a professional one and therefore a habitual one. Though she hated it, she made her livelihood by catering to the cravings of Hebrew and Roman men alike, and thoroughly believed that she could not survive without the more-than-sufficient income she acquired from her chosen profession.

And yet that horrible word…

Sinner!

---

[50] Character not named in the Bible. Name added to enrich story.

Appropriate as it was, it labeled her with an identity that carved her soul into tiny pieces.

But this morning was different. She had slept well the night before, a gift from one of her longtime clients. It was still light the previous day when he knocked.

"Gerah!" she said in a mesh of surprise and annoyance. "Are you mad? You know not to come to me before the sun goes down." He just stood there. "What's wrong with you?" Without waiting for an answer, Neriah pulled him into the house. "Now, what is this all about?"

Gerah looked mesmerized. "I am not sure."

"Come, Gerah, the sun has overcome you. Sit on my bed." She led him there. "Give me a moment," Neriah said, "while I put some perfume on." She turned toward her alabaster jar of ointment.

"No, Neriah. You do not have to."

She faced him. "Then why are you here? And what is wrong with you?"

Gerah took a deep breath to gather himself, his eyes distant. "Tell me, Neriah," he said, with words unsteady, "have you ever heard about the Rabbi from Nazareth? This man called Jesus."

"Of course I have. Just about all my clients know him. They see him whenever they travel throughout Galilee. What about him?"

Gerah struggled. "Today, there was a funeral…"

"What about it?"

"A widow… I had seen her in the marketplace."

"Does she have a name?"

"I do not know it. She has a son … had a son … has a son …"

"What are you babbling about, Gerah? Out with it!"

"All right, Neriah. Here it is. I was leaving the marketplace earlier today and came upon a funeral procession. I stepped aside to let it pass and overheard two women talking. The funeral was for an eighteen-year-old young man. The only son of his mother."

"I think I know who you are talking about. May God have mercy on her."

"He did."

Neriah scrunched her face. "What do you mean?"

"Out of nowhere, it seems, the Rabbi Jesus and his men walked up to them. Everything stopped." Neriah was fascinated by Gerah's story. "The Rabbi went straight to the widow and said, 'Do not cry.' He then approached the coffin, placed his hand on it, and said, 'Young man, I say to you, get up!'"

Neriah was stunned. "Next, Neriah, and I swear to this, the young man sat up and began to speak! The men carrying the coffin lowered it and retreated. The boy then rose and embraced his mother."

"Are you dizzy, Gerah? What kind of story is this?"

Unexpectedly, Gerah rushed to her and challenged her face-to-face. "It is the truth, Neriah! I could never have made up such a story. Go to the marketplace now, while it is still light, and you will hear people talking about it."

He released her. "I am not sure why I came, Neriah, but I felt led to tell you."

With that, he walked out the door. Neriah was left alone, startled and shaken. Suddenly, something started rising in her soul that she had not felt for years—hope. "I must see this man tomorrow," she determined in the emptiness of her home.

She knew what she must do. Peace covered her that night as she slept. Rising early the next morning, she felt fully rested and alive. Then the tears started. There was sweet release in her weeping. While she dressed, Neriah concealed herself meticulously, as she had done for years. She knew what would happen if she was recognized in public.

After making her way to the marketplace, disappointment started to slow her steps. Approaching a metalworker with whom she had previously done business, Neriah mustered the courage to speak. "Good morning, sir," she said. "Tell me, have you seen the Rabbi today?"

"You mean the one who raised the young man?" Neriah's heart skipped. "No, he has not been here." Neriah was crushed. "Though," the man continued, "I know where he will be."

"Please tell me, sir."

"Simon the Pharisee invited him to his house for lunch. We all plan to go there to see him."

Neriah turned to leave with new determination. Returning home, she sat on the side of her bed, wondering what to do next. *I must see him! I must.* And yet to enter the house of a Pharisee…

Regardless. She *had* to.

Just before noon, Neriah decided to leave. However, before walking to Simon's home, she had the strangest inclination to remove her heavy garments. Something inside nudged her to present herself to the Rabbi just as she was. She felt strangely emboldened. Walking past her dresser as she left, she eyed an alabaster jar full of precious ointment and took it; she would anoint the Rabbi's head with it.

Soon at Simon's house, her heart began to beat in fear, but she kept going. Neriah could see the looks of disgust on the men's faces as she approached. All the better, because they scrambled, allowing her to pass easily.

Once inside, she looked at the table, and there he was—the Rabbi. She *knew* it was him. Her heart continued to beat ferociously.

As she approached him, she could still feel the hateful glares being slung at her, but she was undaunted. She no longer felt any shame. Her goal was the Rabbi. As she reached him, he looked up at her and smiled. Seeing he was eating, she knew she could not anoint his head, but noticed that he was reclining, his feet extended away from him.

Neriah came to his feet and kneeled. A sudden wave of emotion overcame her, and she began weeping uncontrollably. Her tears began to drench the Rabbi's feet, and Neriah dried them with her hair. The Rabbi made no attempt to stop her. She opened the alabaster jar and began to pour some perfume on his feet, wipe them with her hair, then repeat the process. She had never felt such peace in her life, and yet her tears kept spilling out of her.

She then heard the Rabbi speak. "Simon," he said, "I have something to tell you."

"Please speak, Rabbi."

"Simon, two men owed money to a certain moneylender. One owed him five hundred denarii, and the other fifty. Neither could pay him back, so he canceled the debts of both. Which of them will love him more?"

Neriah felt the words pierce her, reaching deep into her soul and releasing her from her long years of sinful bondage.

"I suppose the one who had the bigger debt canceled," Simon said grudgingly.

"You have judged correctly," Jesus said. Then Jesus suddenly sat up and looked directly at Neriah. She felt as if she would explode as her heart began beating even more furiously. "Do you see this woman?" Jesus said, still addressing the Pharisee. "I came into your house. You did not give me any water for my feet, but she wet my feet with her tears and wiped them with her hair. From the time I entered, she has not stopped kissing my feet. Therefore, I tell you, her many sins have been forgiven."

Neriah froze at the shocking proclamation. Abruptly, her heart stopped racing. It was tranquil, at peace. Jesus then smiled at her. "Your sins, woman, are forgiven."

Neriah shuddered, her euphoric soul shouting within her, but her tongue was unable to speak.

And as if to make sure she fully understood, the Rabbi said it again. "Your faith has saved you, dear woman, go in peace."

She looked into the Rabbi's eyes and was overcome by the compassion that came flooding out of them. She had difficulty standing, so the Rabbi rose, took her hand, and helped her up. To Neriah, there was only the two of them.

"Go in peace," Jesus assured her.

In wonderful, glorious elation, Neriah quickly found her strength. She began to leave, as the Rabbi had encouraged her to do, and headed to the door. She was oblivious to the hateful stares following her. She felt no shame.

Sinner? No more. The Rabbi had said so. From that day forth, she was His. Her old life was over. Her wicked ways were over. Her days of shame were over.

She would now triumph in the light of the Rabbi's glory—sin and shame a thing of the past.

Neriah and You

Neriah was a "sinful" woman.

The fifteen-verse section (Luke 7:36–50) that speaks about her tells us four times that she was a sinner (vv. 37, 39, 47, 48)—and with it, the deep shame that came from her sinfulness.

What about you? Have you engaged in shameful behavior in your past? You have come to know Christ as your Lord and Savior but still cannot shake the shame of younger days? And, you wonder, *Must I always carry the shame of my past?*

The answer is no!

As God's adopted child through faith in Christ (John 1:12), you "will never be put to shame or disgraced" (Isaiah 45:17). You can feel absolutely free to come before Jesus and say, "In you, O Lord, I have taken refuge; let me never be put to shame; deliver me in your righteousness" (Psalm 31:1).

Notice one common word in both verses: "never." God is clear that if you belong to Him, you will suffer *no* shame. This is not talking about embarrassment. Of course, circumstances in your life may cause you embarrassment—tripping clumsily in front of one hundred people comes to mind—but this is not the kind of shame referred to here. What Isaiah and King David are referring to is the shame and disgrace of sin. Sin comes in many forms and some—humanly speaking—are worse than others. For instance, yelling out a wrong word when you're cut off in traffic does not carry the same consequences as years of sexual promiscuity. The so-called shame of the first passes quickly; that of the latter often lingers for years.

And yet the Lord is adamant: "See, I lay in Zion a stone that causes men to stumble and a rock that makes them fall, and the one who trusts in him will *never* be put to shame" (Romans 9:33, italic added). Again, the "shame" being referred to here is sin, and God says that the shed blood of Christ on the cross has removed your shame and sin.

But you may be asking, *Why is this so?*

The answer is simple: "Therefore, there is now no condemnation for those who are in Christ Jesus" (Romans 8:1). Shame can only come when there is condemnation for sin. Remove the condemnation and shame flees. This is exactly what happened with you when you gave your life to Christ. Condemnation vanished and with it your shame. Additionally, your "former self," which committed such sinful acts, no longer exists. In 2 Corinthians 5:17, you are told, "If anyone is in Christ, he [or she] is a new creation; the old has gone, the new has come!" In other words, the person you *were* is dead!

And that's pretty final. So, where is shame? Where is disgrace? You lived a pretty sinful life, huh? Well, guess what? That life is dead and buried. And with it your shame.

In accepting Christ as your Savior, you have banished shame. Once and for all!

Mary Magdalene
OVERCOMING WORTHLESSNESS

—«»—

"**W**orthless!"

"You have no purpose!"

"Why do you not you just drown yourself and end your misery!"

The once-familiar taunts had suddenly resurfaced, rising somewhere from the deeper recesses of her consciousness. The good thing—if there was something good about this sudden emergence of past torments—was that the voice she was hearing was her own and not the demons who once controlled her.

For the most part, however, this new development in Mary's life was puzzling. After all, she had been washed clean, healed, and saved. Why the sudden bout of doubt, panic, and fear?

Mary's trip back to her home village of Magdala was more difficult than she ever imagined it would be. And that baffled her. She had been made new by Jesus, and had even been the first person He appeared to following His resurrection. This alone should have been enough to calm her anxieties. But it was something about this village, this Magdala, nestled snugly on the western shore of the Sea of Galilee, that so ruffled her. It was now a month following Christ's resurrection, and she had come home to share with her former neighbors all that had happened over the past three years.

However, her first trip back home had taken a very dark and disagreeable turn. And that was strange, because things did not start off that way when she arrived the day before. In fact, all went well at first when she returned to her childhood home and joyfully greeted her parents. It was wonderful to see them again, and she rejoiced in doing so. She also felt fine as she circulated throughout the small village, saying hello to former friends and acquaintances and telling anyone who would listen about the man from Nazareth called Jesus.

But it was that first night, as she lay in her old bed in her old room, that things began to go askew. The great euphoria she had been experiencing the past month had vanished, and it was replaced by confusion and discomfort. Mary could not figure out why.

She rose early the next morning just before dawn and walked down to the shore of Galilee, where the fishermen were arriving after their night's catches out on the sea. Clasping her hands firmly as if praying, Mary began to meander along the coastline, trying to make sense of the calamity that was beginning to overrun her mind and her sudden feelings of worthlessness and despair.

As she started mulling over this disagreeable development, Mary decided to return to the beginning of her troubles, allowing her mind to travel back to the years before she met Jesus. She recalled her youth, which was typical and without incident. When she reached age thirteen, her parents tried to arrange a marriage for her, but they rarely could find a suitable match for their industrious daughter. And when they did manage to stumble over one, they could tell that Mary was simply not interested in being a bride.

Fortunately for the young teenager, her parents, though strongly insisting, never forced their daughter to marry anyone she did not feel comfortable with. And so she was able to hold on to her singleness and her independence. By age eighteen, Mary had become a fixture in the marketplace of Magdala, selling beautiful garments—tunics, robes, and nightclothes she had woven—and was quite a successful woman. By the age of twenty-two, and still living at home, she had accrued a somewhat small fortune. Life was good.

In a world where men dominated, Mary had managed to carve out her own niche—her own little piece of the universe where she could support herself and live independently of her parents should her father die. But more than anything, Mary was bursting with self-confidence and worth—and not in a vain way. On the contrary, she was quite humble by nature but took pride in the fact of knowing that no matter what, she would always be able to stand on her own.

And then something horrible happened.

One evening, as she and her parents were sharing dinner, she felt a jolt in her body. She could not explain what it was, but it seemed as if something had come crashing into her. She felt violated and grew wildly fearful. She looked up at her parents and could see they were staring at her.

Then all went black.

When she regained her senses, she looked around the room and noticed that it was in shambles. Plates were broken, food scattered everywhere, and cushions were torn. She looked down at her hands. They were bleeding. She felt winded and dizzy.

She looked up at her parents to ask them what had just happened, but she was left mute by the sight of her mother cowering in her father's embrace. He had scratches on his face and arms and his hair was disheveled, as if he had been in a fight.

"A demon, Mary…" he stammered.

"What?" she asked woozily.

"A demon, my daughter, has come into you," he said, his voice trembling while his wife sobbed. "I am afraid, my love, you are possessed."

That was the beginning of a four-year nightmare that would torment Mary and her family. Two days following the incident, the voices began. *"Mary, you are unworthy to live,"* one would say. *"No one loves you or needs you,"* another echoed in all its wretched fury.

As her mind grew more afflicted, she became incapable of carrying out daily activities. Within three months, her demon possession had become so severe that she was forced to shut down her thriving business. But worse than anything, she could not be left alone. To do so would be to condemn her to the will of the demons, who would surely cause her to kill herself. Life became ghastly for her parents, and during Mary's rare moments of lucidity, she could see that in just a few short years, constantly keeping vigil over her was taking a toll on them as they aged cruelly.

And all along, the horrific voices continued to plague her. *"Why do you not walk into the lake and drown yourself?"* one would urge. A different demon would try to entice her to fling herself into any fire she saw burning.

She eventually came to understand that her body had become the lodging of seven demons. The rabbis and holy men of Galilee were helpless against them. There would be times of insanity followed by tranquility, then back to insanity. Mary became hideous to look at during those times—her hair a mop of stringy disarray, her eyes bulged and frightening, her cheeks sunken and gaunt.

Her parents tried to keep her indoors during her fits of frenzy, but they were not strong enough. Whenever she went into her rants—usually in the marketplace—the terrorized citizens of Magdala would scatter. Life was agony.

She even began believing the vile accusations. "I am worthless. I have no value. I bring nothing but gloom and terror to all who love me. What purpose is there in me living?"

Her parents sooner or later found themselves struggling to give her a positive answer.

Then one day, during a bout of insanity, she saw a man and his followers enter the marketplace. Instantly, her demonic tenants dragged her to him and began spewing words of hatred and revilement against him. But the man would have none of it. He raised his hand and demanded, "Demons, leave this woman at once!"

Mary fell to the ground, as if dead.

When she opened her eyes, the first thing she saw was the smiling face of the man who had healed her. His countenance spoke volumes of love and compassion to her, the likes of which she never knew existed. From that day forth, she was His. She would accompany His small band of followers and provide for their needs out of the abundance she had accumulated over the years. She would witness His miracles and learn at His feet. She would also witness His death on the cross—and was crushed.

But that was only momentary, because He revealed Himself to her following His resurrection. He told her to tell the disciples that she had seen Him. She did and she did not stop there. She came home to Magdala to tell those who had once held her in such contempt. Returning to this place of such terrible memories, however, had jolted her, but she at last figured out what was happening.

"Satan," she said aloud, "you have no more hold over me. I belong to Jesus the Lord. Be gone from me! I have worth! I have a place!"

Suddenly, a profound peace fell upon her. All dark contemplation was vanquished. She would never again allow her mind to play games on her. The chilling thoughts of worthlessness she had once felt were over and done with, never to rise again.

She belonged totally to Jesus and would belong to Him for eternity.

Mary Magdalene and You

Feeling worthless and unwanted is the pits! Mary Magdalene knew what it was like.

Chances are, so do you. It is a terrible burden to carry.

If events of your past—whether inflicted by someone or something other than you, as was the case with Mary, or of your own doing—continue to torment you with feelings of unworthiness, you are not alone. But, to be quite frank, if you know Jesus Christ as your Lord and Savior, here's a loving encouragement: you should never have to feel this way.

First, consider your worth and value to God: "Fear not, for I have redeemed you; I have summoned you by name; you are mine" (Isaiah 43:1). In context, these words were spoken to ancient Israel, God's chosen people. As a believer in Christ, you are also one of God's chosen (1 Peter 2:9). As such, you are His! In other words, you are God's very possession. Note the passion, the tenacity with which God makes this assertion: "I have summoned you by name [insert your own name here], you are mine"

Second, notice that God has a specific purpose for you. Ephesians 2:10 says, "For we are God's workmanship, created in Christ Jesus to do good works, which God prepared in advance for us to do." Still feeling worthless? This verse simply will not permit it! Not only did God call you as His very special possession, but He also has a specific purpose for you to achieve. He has appointed you to do something for Him that only you can do. There's no room—or place—for feelings of worthlessness. At least, not in God's eyes.

Third, you accept all this, but you still can't get over your past. Here's good news for you—God wants you to get over it: "...at that time you were separate from Christ, excluded from citizenship in Israel and [a] foreigner to the covenants of the promise, without hope and without God in the world. But now in Christ Jesus you who once were far away have been brought near through the blood of Christ" (Ephesians 2:12–13). So, do you "have a past," as the expression goes? No big deal. God has brought you near to Him through the blood of Christ. Were you at one time worthless? Spiritually speaking, yes. But now? Not on your life!

Fourth, as a child of God, you have a mandate: "For you were once darkness, but now you are light in the Lord. Live as children of light...and find out what pleases the Lord" (Ephesians 5:8, 10). Notice the phrases, "you were once" and "but now." That's God's way of telling you that the past is over; your new existence is all that matters.

While demon possessed, Mary Magdalene was useless. But once Christ entered her life, she became invaluable to Him. You, too, are invaluable to Jesus. You have a divine purpose of great worth. Now find out what it is and accomplish it!

Nicodemus

OVERCOMING CULTURAL PRESSURE

→«»→

The unexpected knock on the door stirred Nicodemus from his sleep.

It was still dark. He slowly steered his aging legs from the bed, rose deliberately, and stumbled toward the door. There stood a young man, eighteen at best, his face carved in urgency.

"Yes," Nicodemus said politely. "You have a message for me?"

"I do, sir." Nicodemus nodded for him to continue. "The Sanhedrin has been summoned to meet in one hour. I was sent to inform you."

"Do you know why we are meeting?" he asked.

"It is about the crucified Rabbi from Nazareth."

"What about him?"

"Reports are circulating around Jerusalem that he has…"

"Yes?"

"Well," the teen stuttered, "his followers claim that he has…risen…from the dead."

Nicodemus's heart skipped a beat, and he struggled to calm himself. "When?"

"Well, sir, according to them, when several of their party went to visit his tomb yesterday morning, it was empty."

Nicodemus knew the tomb well.

"And then, sir," the youngster continued, "some of his followers reported that he had come to visit them."

Nicodemus's heart thundered. "Very well," he told the messenger, "you have been most helpful. Thank you."

Nicodemus closed the door and staggered back to his bedroom, his movements halting, his thoughts cluttered. And yet, as he sat on his bed, he realized that he was smiling. Then almost involuntarily, he found himself saying, "I believe it, Lord. I believe it."

A truly uncharacteristic affirmation of faith.

Among Jerusalem's finest teachers, Nicodemus was a Pharisee, or "separated one." These self-proclaimed keepers of the laws of Moses were keenly zealous for purity and ritual. Often, they carried their pious passion too far, imposing on the people of Israel interpretations of laws they conjured themselves, and these extra-scriptural statutes became a burden for the people to bear.

But Nicodemus was not one to oppress the common man spiritually with unjust renditions of the law. He believed it was enough for his fellow Israelites to revere God and love one another without loading them down with impossible decrees. For Nicodemus, loving God and serving Him were the epitome of Jewish obedience, and he strove to do so the best he could.

He also sought to teach others the same, and, as a master instructor, was in an ideal position to do just that. Because of his matchless wisdom and compassion, Nicodemus was revered by the people of Jerusalem and highly respected by his fellow Pharisees, a rare honor among the six thousand of them scattered throughout Israel. And when his acclaim reached its peak, he was invited to join the elite collection of seventy-one men who made up the Sanhedrin, Israel's primary civil and judiciary body. To put it all in perspective, Nicodemus represented everything that was good about Israel and Judaism.

And then came the Rabbi from Nazareth.

As Nicodemus rose from his bed and began to dress in the black flowing garments of Sanhedrin members, he replayed the young messenger's words: "His followers claim he has risen from the dead."

And without intending to, he found himself saying aloud, "Just as He said He would."

The words caught the elderly gentleman by surprise, and once again he smiled, though his heart was racing. He was amazed at the ease with which he expressed such faith.

However, it was not always like that.

When word of Jesus first started circulating in Jerusalem three years earlier, Nicodemus's Pharisee and Sanhedrin brothers derisively scoffed at His followers' claims that He was a teacher sent from God—the Messiah, the Son of God.

Nicodemus believed the first assertion, but the second and third? The Messiah? The Son of God? However, he adamantly refused to join in the vicious barbs, jeers, and scathing sarcasm so freely spewed from the lips of his peers. It was not in him to act in such a way. It was not his style. And besides that, there was one issue that simply could not be ignored by the Sanhedrin: the miracles.

Oh yes, they were real and undeniable. Thousands of people had witnessed them. The Pharisees and Sanhedrin included. The blind *were* healed. The lame *did* walk. The sick *were* made well. The dead *did* come back to life. Undeniable. But who gave the Galilean power to achieve such feats? Nicodemus's peers said it came from Satan. Nicodemus *knew* it came from God.

When he spoke on Jesus' behalf, his peers cut him down, calling him foolish for allowing himself to become so easily bamboozled by the wily wizard of Nazareth. "I will speak with him myself and find out about him from his own mouth," he told them.

"Watch yourself, Nicodemus," they warned. "He is crafty and will draw you in. We do not approve of him and would be disappointed if you conclude differently. In fact, we *strongly* suggest that you stay away from him—unless several of us accompany you."

Nicodemus dropped the matter, until that evening. Not wanting to be caught "fraternizing with the enemy," Nicodemus now stood alone with the Man who was more than half his age. And yet, as the esteemed gentleman stood gazing at Him, he felt like a child, his years of wisdom, learning, and knowledge obliterated by the Rabbi's divine-like authority.

"Rabbi," Nicodemus ventured, trying not to cower before the Nazarene, "we know you are a teacher who has come from God.

For no one could perform the miraculous signs you are doing if God were not with him."

Jesus smiled and placed His hand on the older man's shoulder. His touch was firm but warm, and it signaled to Nicodemus that He was to be attentive. The Rabbi had no intention of explaining to him who He was. He already knew that Nicodemus sensed it.

"I tell you the truth," the Rabbi said, his words kind but saturated with authority, "no one can see the kingdom of God unless he is born again."

Nicodemus struggled with the meaning of the odd statement, but he also felt his heart torn in two. The Rabbi had cut straight through to His soul. "How can a man be born when he is old?" Nicodemus stammered. "Surely, he cannot enter a second time into his mother's womb to be born!"

The conversation would continue. In essence, Jesus told Nicodemus that though a good man and born Jewish, he had no more claim to eternal life than did the most vile of Gentiles. Nicodemus was disarmed, shot down, humbled, laid bare, and his weakness was revealed. He lacked spiritual discernment, lacked faith. All his knowledge had led him nowhere—until now. Until this one-sided showdown with the Rabbi, *the... Messiah.*

Nicodemus teetered as he returned home. He remained in a haze for a week. *Who is this man?* he wondered over and again. *How could he have pierced my soul as He did? Why do my peers hate him as they do? He is no heretic.*

A year later, Nicodemus discovered that he was not alone. A fellow Sanhedrin member, Joseph of Arimathea, sensing Nicodemus's reverence for the Rabbi, revealed to him that he, too, shared the same reverence. "But we dare not speak our minds to our brothers," Joseph cautioned. "They will have us barred from the synagogue."

Nicodemus agreed. The cultural pressure placed on them by the Jewish leadership was unbearable, and they could not stand under the weight of it. Too much was at stake. They would lose their position and status.

But then, another year later, came the unlawful trial of Jesus of Nazareth—the disgraceful and unjust death decree of an innocent man.

Joseph approached Nicodemus. "I can remain silent no longer, my brother," he said, tears falling. "We must bury Him. I have a tomb."

"But we will lose everything," Nicodemus objected weakly.

"We will lose even more if we remain silent."

Nicodemus felt his heart being shredded. Together they approached the Roman governor Pilate and requested for Jesus' body so they could bury it. Pilate consented. Together they watched mortified as Jesus died on the cross. And when it was over, with their peers watching them, they claimed His lifeless body and carried it off. They ignored the icy stares stabbing them like poison daggers as they anointed Jesus' body with expensive spices and wrapping it in strips of linen.

From the moment they took His body, Nicodemus and Joseph were exposed for what they were: believers in Jesus Christ, the Son of God. It was all out in the open now. They were caught red-handed.

And now, as Nicodemus closed the door behind him and made his way to the meeting of the Sanhedrin, he knew he would discover what would become of him. He had stood up to the oppressive cultural pressure that threatened to bury him in social darkness, and he had triumphed over its menace.

Nothing the Sanhedrin did to him now mattered. Jesus had risen from the dead. He was alive! The world was about to change.

Nicodemus would never fear again.

Nicodemus and You

It takes a lot to stand up against the culture.

It was extremely difficult for Nicodemus, and it is just as difficult for you. Being a Christian in today's hostile world is daunting. What with being bombarded by philosophies and beliefs that blatantly oppose what the Bible teaches. If you are single and want to remain pure, the world tells you to sleep with whomever you want. If you are married and want to remain faithful, the world tells you to have an affair. If you want to avoid the coarse and distasteful, the world tells you to watch that movie or TV show.

Living according to God's holy commands is ridiculed in this dark world, and doing so often comes at a price. Being ostracized by your family and friends could well be one of them.

And yet Jesus said, "Whoever acknowledges me before men, I will also acknowledge him before my Father in heaven. But whoever disowns me before men, I will disown him before my Father in heaven" (Matthew 10:32–33). Seems rather harsh, doesn't it? If someone asks you to go to a bar with them, you could just say no, but Jesus would have you say something like, "I cannot dishonor God by going into such a place."

You already know the ridicule that awaits such a reply. The Bible tells you that your acquaintances will "think it strange that you do not plunge with them into the same flood of dissipation, and they heap abuse on you" (1 Peter 4:4). Not much fun to think about.

Instead, you are urged to "come out from them and be separate" (1 Corinthians 6:17). And you may well be separated. Taking a stand for Christ—overcoming cultural pressure—is not for the squeamish. In fact, far from indulging yourself in the sinfulness of the culture, you are called upon to: "Give thanks to the Lord, call on his name; make known among the nations what he has done. Sing to him, sing praise to him; tell of all his wonderful acts" (Psalm 105:1–2).

And you thought it was difficult enough just to keep away from those things which offend God. Now you see that the Lord wants you to proclaim Him to all you come in contact with. You can almost imagine how *that's* going to work out for you.

So, what's the bottom line? What did Nicodemus gain from proclaiming Christ? What will you gain from standing up to the cultural pressure that is oppressing you?

It's this: at the end of your life, you, like The apostle Paul, will be able to say: "I have fought the good fight, I have finished the race, I have kept the faith. Now there is in store for me the crown of righteousness, which the Lord, the righteous Judge, will award to me on that day" (2 Timothy 4:7–8).

There is no greater triumph than this!

The Greek Woman

OVERCOMING BARRIERS

←❖→

How Phoebe,[51] just this once, wished that she were born Jewish.

"Oh, my love," she tearfully pleaded with her suffering daughter, "hang on just a little longer. Deliverance *will* come. I am certain of it."

In response, Prisca turned to her mother and spit at her. It was not the first time it had happened. No, not in the year since her now fourteen-year-old daughter suddenly, frighteningly, dropped the dinner tray she was carrying one evening and fell to the floor in a shocking spasm of such force that Phoebe and her husband could only cower. It all happened so fast, and when it was over, poor Prisca could barely move. A visit from the physician did nothing to reveal the mystery of the strange episode, which made sense because there was nothing he could have done.

About a week later, on a chilly morning, while Phoebe and Prisca were in the marketplace of Tyre, a Mediterranean seaport

---

[51] Character not named in the Bible. Name added to enrich story.

city, Phoebe saw a fire burning. Its purpose was to warm the hands of merchants and shoppers alike. Phoebe stopped when she noticed that Prisca had done the same and wondered what on earth she was staring at. Then, just as suddenly as the spasm had attacked her the previous week, so did Prisca's next shocking action.

Phoebe watched in horror as Prisca abruptly began sprinting toward the fire, around which three men were gathered. As one of them saw Prisca's mad dash in his direction, he stepped aside just in time as the girl incomprehensibly flung herself into the flames!

Phoebe fell to her knees in dread, her face ashen. Fortunately for both her and her daughter, the men, allowing for a moment or two of dazed paralysis, gathered their wits and at once hauled the deranged girl from the blaze. Their quick work prevented any serious injury to Prisca, but her condition was clear: she was possessed by a demon—whose sole purpose was to destroy the girl in the most abominable manner imaginable.

For a full year, Phoebe and her husband would have to keep constant vigil on their daughter for those moments when the demon within her struck. To turn their back for a moment could spell the end of their precious daughter's life.

Phoebe sought help from the pagan priests who littered the Mediterranean landscape, but they were helpless to combat this—*thing*—that had infiltrated Prisca. Phoebe and her husband's lives had become misery, the enormity of their daughter's affliction wearing them down and aging them beyond their years.

Then, about a month previous, a neighbor merchant returning from Capernaum, about thirty miles away in northern Israel, rushed into the family home while they were eating. "Phoebe," he gushed breathlessly. "I have found a man who can cure Prisca."

She and her husband stared at each other in disbelief, then turned back to their neighbor. "What are you talking about?" Phoebe asked incredulously.

"A Rabbi from Nazareth...I saw it with my own eyes."

"Saw what?" Phoebe's husband asked impatiently.

"He heals...miraculously. I saw it. I witnessed it. The blind, the lame—he healed them all."

From Prisca's bedroom, the couple could hear the sleeping girl beginning to stir. The neighbor continued. "But beyond this...I swear to the truth of what I am about to tell you...this man cast out demons. Many of them. Those who were demon-possessed walked away as whole and healed, as if nothing had ever happened."

They heard Prisca rise from the bed.

"This man...his name...what is it?" Phoebe asked desperately, rising to her feet and coming to within inches of the messenger's face.

"They called him Jesus."

They heard Prisca scream out an expletive.

"Tell us more about this man. Quickly!"

"His followers claim he is the Messiah of Israel...the very son of God."

Phoebe was stupefied. "The son of God? How can this be?"

But before another word could be spoken, Prisca suddenly rushed from the room. "Curses on this man! Curses on those who speak his name!"

She ran to attack the neighbor, but Phoebe intercepted her and was at once joined by her husband.

"Tell me," Phoebe continued while subduing her daughter, "whom did he heal?"

"What do you mean?"

"Did he heal people … like us?"

"No," her neighbor sadly replied, "just the Jews."

There was silence as Phoebe and her husband at last quelled their daughter's short-lived outburst.

For the following month, this Rabbi of Capernaum became Phoebe's new obsession. But could she reach him? A heathen, she began praying to the Jewish God. But would He listen? She cursed the vile gulf, that infernal barrier that separated Jews and Gentiles!

Then early one morning, the neighbor who had first told her of the Rabbi came pounding on her door. "He is here! The Rabbi!"

Phoebe's heart began to race. "Where?"

"In the inn. You will find him there."

"But I cannot leave Prisca alone."

"Wait here. I will get my wife to watch her."

Phoebe ran into Prisca's room; her daughter was foaming at the mouth and had just spit at her.

"God of the Jews," Phoebe prayed, "please allow my daughter to hold on."

When her neighbor's wife arrived, there were no greetings, just urgency. "Go now, Phoebe! Hurry!"

"But will he help a Gentile?"

"He is here—in heathen territory—is he not?"

It was enough for Phoebe as she bolted from her home and sprinted the quarter-mile to the inn just outside the marketplace. She raced past the reception area and ignored the innkeeper's attempts to stop her. She instinctively made her way to the dining room where she saw a group of men—Jewish men, Galileans.

She gazed at them and they at her, as if she were defiling them. She caught sight of one particular man; he was looking down at his plate. She knew. There was no time to waste.

"Lord, Son of David"—she knew enough about Jewish beliefs to refer to him by his Messianic title—"have mercy on me! My daughter is suffering terribly from demon possession."

The Rabbi did not acknowledge her. She cried out again. Silence. She cried out again. The Rabbi's men were growing impatient. "Send her away," they urged, their annoyance evident, "for she keeps crying out after us."

At this, the Rabbi looked up at Phoebe. "I was sent only to the lost sheep of Israel." His words were soft, his manner gentle.

There was no time to lose. Phoebe ran to him and flung herself at his feet. She had never felt like such an unclean Gentile in her life. "Lord, help me!" she begged on the verge of hysterics.

"It is not right to take the children's bread and toss it to their dogs."

Though sounding like a terrible insult, coming from him it was nothing of the sort. His words were filled with tranquility and love—an invitation rather than a rebuke.

Phoebe felt empowered. And she understood. "Yes," she concurred, "you have come to bring blessings to your people. I do not wish to rob them. I only ask for my suffering daughter. Oh, Lord, please … please …"

The Rabbi's face was serene, tender … merciful. Phoebe was bursting. "Yes," she sobbed, "I *am* a dog. But even the dogs eat the crumbs that fall from their masters' table. I ask you only for a crumb."

At this, the Rabbi's face radiated with compassion. "Woman, you have great faith!" he declared.

He moved closer to her. "Your request is granted. For such a reply, you may go; the demon has left your daughter."

At that moment, Phoebe felt the oppressive burden wonderfully rise from her. She looked at the Rabbi and wanted to thank him, but the words simply would not—could not—come.

"Go to her, dear woman," the Rabbi urged softly. "Go to her."

Phoebe rose slowly and gave the Rabbi one final look of gratitude, then turned quickly and ran home, invigorated as never before. At her arrival, her neighbor's wife ran out of Prisca's room to greet her. She was about to speak but could not.

Her face was covered in tears.

Phoebe knew. She raced to Prisca's room and stopped. At the sight of her, Prisca rose to a sitting position and held out her arms. "Mother."

It was the sweetest sound Phoebe had ever heard. She rushed to her daughter's waiting arms and exultantly returned the embrace. As mother and daughter rejoiced in this unfathomable moment, Phoebe began to sob uncontrollably, with Prisca doing the same.

Thank you, dear Lord, Phoebe's soul spoke, expressing words she had no strength to speak. *You have listened to this dog of a woman. You have broken down the barrier that has separated me from You. I will worship You always.*

In the glory of the moment, neither Phoebe nor Prisca had any intention of terminating their embrace any time soon.

The Greek Woman and You

We can only imagine the incredible fear Phoebe felt as she approached Jesus.

It is not that she doubted Jesus' ability to heal her daughter; rather, she feared the barrier that separated them—He was a Jew and she was a Gentile. And the two didn't mix. This religious barrier was a serious threat to her daughter's well-being, but Phoebe was willing to overcome it.

What about you? What barrier keeps you from worshiping God as you should? Is it religion? Are you from a Jewish background? Muslim? Cultic? Satanic worship? If this is the case, here's a newsflash: IT DOESN'T MATTER!

That's right. Listen to the words of the apostle Paul: "But now in Christ Jesus you who once were far away have been brought near through the blood of Christ. For he himself is our peace, who has made the two one and has destroyed *the barrier*, the dividing wall of hostility, by abolishing in his flesh the law with its commandments and regulations. His purpose was to create in himself one new man out of the two, thus making peace" (Ephesians 2:13–15, emphasis added).

In context, this verse is specifically speaking about the gulf between Jews and Gentiles. But it also implies something much more than just these two divisions. The religious barrier—and let's include atheism and agnosticism—that once separated you from God has been obliterated by the shed blood of Jesus Christ.

Paul further emphasizes this truth elsewhere when he writes: "…for all of you who were baptized into Christ have clothed yourselves with Christ. There is neither Jew nor Greek, slave nor free, male nor female, for you are all one in Christ Jesus" (Galatians 3:27–29). Do you see any barriers here? Of course not. Though Paul did not have time to include every barrier imaginable, he certainly implied it. Other barriers keeping you from God that were destroyed on the cross are your country of origin and the family you grew up in.

In other words, it doesn't matter what part of the world you were raised in; who your father, mother, or siblings are; what religion—or no religion at all—you once were; what your social or financial status is; or whether or not you have ever cursed the name of God. There are *no* barriers that will keep you from Christ. None.

Phoebe, a Greek woman living in Syrian Phoenicia (modern-day Lebanon), was a Gentile. As such, she was separated from God.

Even Jesus acknowledged that, though He was making a point. But notice one crucial thing: Jesus *deliberately* took His men up to the Gentile territory (Matthew 15:21). He knew exactly what—or who—awaited Him up there. He was on a mission to heal this Gentile woman's daughter.

And He is on a mission to love you, bless you, and mold you into His image. Do you see any barriers between Him and you?

No? Good, because there aren't any!

Thief on the Cross

OVERCOMING ETERNAL JUDGMENT

Imri's[52] life was almost over. It was time to decide.

He knew what he was: a thief on a cross. But who exactly was this man who hung in the middle between him and his fellow thief who was condemned to die with him? Imri heard the insults: "He saved others," the Jewish leaders shouted, "let him save himself if he is the Christ of God; the chosen one."[53] The Christ—the Messiah—of God? *What does that mean?* Imri wondered.

"If you are the king of the Jews," the Romans taunted, "save yourself."[54] The king of the Jews? *Is this man the king of my people?*

"You who are going to destroy the temple and build it in three days, save yourself!" the crowd ridiculed. "Come down from the cross if you are the Son of God."[55] *The Son of God?*

---

[52] Character not named in the Bible. Name added to enrich story.
[53] Luke 23:35
[54] Luke 23:37
[55] Matthew 27:40

Imri's life was slowly ebbing away, the excruciating pain ripping through his body unlike anything he ever imagined. Though seeking a quick end to his misery, he suddenly found himself not as anxious to depart this life. *Who was this man in the middle? Why are so many people hostile toward him, especially now that he, too, has been condemned? Is he a king? The Messiah? God, who is this man!*

It was time for Imri to decide, and he had to decide rightly. After all, a wrong decision five years ago had led him to this point.

Growing up in northern Israel, Imri and his younger brother were the only children of their industrious parents. Though they loved each other deeply, they differed in so many ways, two of them being religion and politics. Imri could remember his teen years and those lively discussions around the dinner table.

"Father," his brother would say, "I keep hearing talk about the Messiah. Who is this Messiah and why do so many people speak of him?"

"The Messiah, son," his father would answer, his creased brow reflecting the magnitude of the issue, "is Israel's savior. He is the one who will come and bring us a new age of peace and power."

"Then why has he not come yet, Father?" Imri would challenge. "With the Romans making our lives miserable, would now not be the perfect time?"

At this, Imri's mother cautioned her husband. "Dear, please be careful what you say. Do not incite the boys."

"Better they should know the truth than be naive."

"I have got things to do inside!" she would say, angrily rising, making no effort to conceal her disgust.

"What is wrong with Mother?" Imri's brother asked.

"She will be fine," his father said, dismissing the question. "But here is the answer to the question. The reason the Messiah has not come yet is because we are not worthy of him."

"Why do you say this, Father?" Imri asked.

"Because our people our cowards. We refuse to stand up to the Romans. We have let them come into our land and have their way with us, and we pander to their every wish. We are embarrassments to God, and until we take courage and act like men, He will never send us the Messiah!"

Such talk ignited Imri's soul. *He is right! We are an unworthy people. But not me! I will stand up! I will fight the Romans!*

When Imri was nineteen, his father died. Not wishing to anguish his bereaved mother any further, he stayed home for a year, unwilling to deprive her of both husband and oldest son at once. But after a year, he had decided. Imri sat his mother down, took both her hands in his, and announced that he was moving to Jerusalem to pursue "spiritual" endeavors.

Imri could tell that she did not believe a word he said. And rightly so.

From the time Imri arrived in the holy city, he found his way to a group called the Zealots, a rabid political faction of Jewish rebels who through violence sought to free the nation from Rome's oppressive hand. They did this several ways. At the most extreme level, a group of one hundred or more of the better-trained Zealots would hide among the rocks and trees as smaller bands of Roman soldiers marched through the land. Whenever the numbers were in their favor, the Zealots would attack these smaller bands of soldiers and destroy them.

Imri stayed away from this dangerous faction and instead favored the more "practical" sector of Zealots. Knowing how important commerce and individual safety were to the Roman Empire, the faction Imri joined would form bands of robbers that roamed Israel from north to south. Whenever encountering foreign traders, Imri and his cohorts would attack them and steal their goods. They had no interest in harming their victims, just in stripping them of their possessions. By making the roads dangerous for visitors, traders would be dissuaded from entering Israel and doing business with Rome.

After five years of such dangerous activity, of which Imri became quite proficient, he was finally caught and arrested, the victim of a Roman stakeout, and he and a fellow Zealot were sentenced to death by crucifixion.

As he was forced to carry the crossbeam upon which he would be crucified, Imri was placed directly behind a man whom people were calling "Jesus," "King of the Jews," "Messiah," and the "Son of God." The man was a horrid mess of blood and tattered skin, the victim of a merciless Roman scourging. How he was even alive, Imri had no idea. And despite the man's frailness, Imri could not take his eyes off him, for even in torment he carried himself with dignity and honor.

When they arrived at the hill of crucifixion, Golgotha, the one called Jesus was crucified first and hung on the cross. Imri was next. As the nails came smashing through his wrists, he heard something extraordinary. From behind him, Jesus said, "Father, forgive them, for they do not know what they are doing."[56]

Imri was amazed and stunned. *Forgive them? How could he say such a thing? Who is this man!*

As the hours passed and Imri studied Jesus on the cross, he kept mulling all that he had heard about him and wondered. *Who is he? Who is he?* Then, around noon, when the sun was high and bright, the sky suddenly began to turn dark. It was an eerie darkness, for there were no clouds, wind, or dust storms. It was a darkness he had never seen before. A... *blue* darkness, one in which the sun was still in the sky.

Imri studied the sky, and then looked at Jesus. *This strange darkness,* he reasoned, *is all because of him. But how? Why? Why such an odd darkness at midday? How could he ask God to forgive those who were killing him? Why did the Jews call him "the Christ"? Why did the Romans call him "the king of the Jews"? Why did the Jewish people watching the crucifixion call him "the Son of God"? He asked his "Father" to forgive them all. His Father? The Son of God? The Messiah?*

---

[56] Luke 23:24

In his scorching agony, Imri continued to ponder, *Who is he? God, please tell me. Who is he? Is he really the Messiah? Is he the one I need to pledge my allegiance to—even now, at the very end?*

His contemplations were rudely interrupted by his companion. "Are you not the Christ?" he sneered at Jesus. "Save yourself and us."[57]

And suddenly, at that moment, it all made sense! The answer is yes! *This is the Christ!*

Imri felt emboldened. "Do you not fear God since you are under the same sentence?" he rebuked his companion. "We are punished justly, for we are getting what our deeds deserve. But this man has done nothing wrong."[58]

And now, without anything holding him back, he spoke to the Messiah. "Jesus," he said, his spirit suddenly renewed, "remember me when you come into your kingdom."[59]

Jesus turned his head toward him, and Imri felt as if time stopped. And though he could not be sure, it appeared to him as if Jesus, if it was even possible, was smiling. "I tell you the truth," he said, his words like rivers of peace cascading through Imri's troubled soul, "today you will be with me in paradise."[60]

At once, Imri had been lifted out of himself. Yes, he was still on the cross, but this was but a technicality. He had heard of this place

---

[57] Luke 23:39
[58] Luke 23:40–41
[59] Luke 23:42
[60] Luke 23:43

"paradise." He knew not what it was but was certain that he would soon be there. And that it would be wonderful. He now welcomed death—awaited it, embraced it—and prayed for it to come quickly.

Heavenly father, he rejoiced in the quiet of his heart, *I have seen your Messiah, Your Son, my Lord and my King. Now, Father, take me to paradise where I may serve Him for eternity! Yes, Lord, take me to blessed paradise!*

Thief on the Cross and You

The thief on the cross came to know Christ at the very end of his life. The thief confessed his belief that Jesus was the Messiah and the One through Whom eternal life is granted. Upon doing so, Jesus assured him that he would soon join Jesus in "paradise," or heaven.

What about if the thief did not confess Christ as Lord? Where would he have gone? Indeed, if you have never confessed Christ as Lord, where are you going?

Here are three facts. One, *all* people are born sinners. The apostle Paul writes: "for all have sinned and fall short of the glory of God" (Romans 3:23). This is an indisputable truth. Two, all sinners face grave consequences. Paul writes, "For the wages of sin is death" (Romans 6:23). The death referred to here is not physical death, but eternal separation from God *after* physical death. Third, the Bible says that "man is destined to die once, and after that to face judgment" (Hebrews 9:27).

This is man's destiny. The question that now needs to be asked is this: what is this "judgment" the book of Hebrews speaks of?

The answer is hell, which the Bible describes as a devastating place of constant torment apart from God. Revelation 20:14–15 says: "Then death and Hades were thrown into the lake of fire. The lake of fire is the second death. If anyone's name was not found written in the book of life, he was thrown into the lake of fire." Though some have questioned whether the phrase "lake of fire" is to be taken literally, there is no reason to doubt. But even if not, the phrase is designed to communicate the idea of damnation, dread, and doom.

This is both the state (sinful) and fate (hell) of natural humanity. Eternal judgment is its sure destiny.

So, what is the solution? How do people overcome such a judgment?

God has provided the way out. Paul writes: "if you confess with your mouth, 'Jesus is Lord,' and believe in your heart that God raised him from the dead, you will be saved" (Romans 10:9). The book of Luke says, "Believe in the Lord Jesus, and you will be saved" (Acts 16:31).

Yes, it is really *that* simple. Salvation in Jesus Christ and deliverance from eternal torment depend on one thing and one only: believing that Jesus Christ is the Son of God, the Messiah, the only One who can save people from their sins. The thief confessed Jesus as Lord and was transported from eternal death to eternal life.

How about you? Have you confessed Jesus as your Lord and Savior? If not, now is the perfect time to get down on your knees and do so. He is waiting to hear from you, just as you are. If you make that confession, then Jesus will smile widely and assure you, "One day, you will be me with me in paradise!"

You can have that assurance today!

Paul

OVERCOMING HATRED

→«»→

"I thank Christ Jesus our Lord, who has given me strength, that he considered me faithful, appointing me to his service. Even though I was once a blasphemer and a persecutor and a violent man, I was shown mercy because I acted in ignorance and unbelief. The grace of our Lord was poured out on me abundantly, along with the faith and love that are in Christ Jesus."[61]

As Paul reread the letter he had just completed to his beloved disciple Timothy, he paused and reconsidered the passage. "Ha, am I really filled abundantly with grace, faith, and love? And all in the name of Jesus, no less!" He laughed aloud.

Paul laughed again. "Who would have thought it? Certainly not me. At least, not in *those* years."

And without much effort, Paul began reflecting on *those* years. Those years when he was not Paul, his Greek name, but Saul, the Hebrew name he was so proud of. And not only that, but he was Saul of Tarsus, circumcised on the eighth day, of the people of Israel, of

---

[61] 1 Timothy 1:12–14

the tribe of Benjamin, a Hebrew of Hebrews. In regard to the law, he was a Pharisee; as for zeal, he was persecuting the church; as for legalistic righteousness, he was faultless.[62]

Yes, he was all of that, and he clung to his resumé with impassioned fortitude. Growing up in the richly diversified city of Tarsus, Paul received the finest of Greek educations and a solid Hebrew one. However, by the time he reached age eighteen, his Pharisee father realized that Paul's Hebrew instruction was inadequate—at least, if his headstrong son was going to follow in his own substantial footprints.

Therefore, Paul's parents packed off their eager offspring and sent him wide-eyed to the Jewish bastion of Jerusalem, where he could complete and perfect his Hebrew education. He would do that, no less, at the feet of the celebrated rabbi Gamaliel, one of the most admired of Jerusalem's religious leaders. Unlike his mentor, however, Paul lacked the levelheadedness and compassion so needed to judge the hearts of his people during these changing times.

Drastically changing times. By the time Paul reached age thirty, he was already set in his ways, ardently adhering to the rigid standards of the most extreme of the Pharisees. His severe views of the Hebrew Scriptures colored every facet of his being, resulting in a pious zeal rarely seen in one so young.

How long ago those years now seemed, as Paul—well past age sixty—was suddenly struck by something he had written years

---

[62] Philippians 3:5–6

earlier. "I want to know Christ and the power of his resurrection and the fellowship of sharing in his sufferings, becoming like him in his death, and so, somehow, to attain to the resurrection from the dead."[63]

Ah, my beloved Lord ... I never thought I would write such words.

Indeed not. From the moment he heard about the so-called Rabbi from Nazareth, Paul knew he was trouble. Just another impostor looking to make a name for himself by stirring up the spiritual fervor of the empty-headed majority of uneducated Israelites, who spread throughout the land like locusts. Paul hated this Galilean masquerader who threatened every tradition, custom, and ritual Paul held dear. Paul knew that this man had to be stopped, and—with his affirmative vote one of many to put the Rabbi to death—he thought that was exactly what the caretakers of the nation had accomplished.

But this did not happen. Some absurd account about the bogus Rabbi rising from the dead on the third day following his crucifixion would stoke the fires of the ignorant masses that much more. Paul could no longer sit idly by. "Let me see to this matter," he said one day, boldly standing before the Sanhedrin, Israel's seventy-one-member supreme ruling body. "I will stamp out his followers one by one if I have to. This sect will gain no stronghold in Jerusalem so long as I breathe."

---

[63] Philippians 3:10–11

Granted with the authorization he so greatly desired, Paul set out to destroy the people of "the Way" and see to it that they would be no more than a distant memory within a year.

"Therefore God exalted him to the highest place and gave him the name that is above every name, that at the name of Jesus every knee should bow, in heaven and on earth and under the earth, and every tongue confess that Jesus Christ is Lord, to the glory of God the Father."[64]

Jesus Christ is Lord, the elderly Paul thought, *I never would have believed it.* Certainly not while carrying out his bloodthirsty assault upon the Way. Though never laying a hand on anyone personally, Paul delighted in ordering the imprisonments of entire families, and never hesitated to decree death sentences against the leaders of the movement.

Then one day, a man a few years younger than he was, one bursting with energy and zeal, was brought before the Sanhedrin on charges of blasphemy. Paul viewed this rebel, this Stephen, with disdain as he stood before the august body of Jewish leaders defending himself. From the moment he was given permission to speak, Stephen launched into such a rousing rendition of the Jewish people's history that even Paul could not help but be swept up by the *blasphemer's* passion and love for God. Paul felt his heart being pierced by Stephen's countenance, which possessed an angelic-like tranquility that tore right through Paul.

---

[64] Philippians 2:9–11

And Paul hated Stephen for radiating a love for God that Paul had no hope of ever attaining. When at last Stephen, his eyes full of tears and wonder, looked up and proclaimed, "I see heaven open and the Son of Man standing at the right hand of God,"[65] Paul believed that his own torment would soon be over. The Jewish leadership, much to Paul's delight, dragged Stephen outside the city and stoned him to death. Paul agreed to watch the garments of the men doing the stoning, but he, too, wished he were hurling stones. And when it was finished, Paul realized that he had partaken in the death of an innocent man who exceeded him in every way.

His mind a muddled mesh of guilt and hatred, Paul attacked the Way as never before, hauling people to prison and ordering executions at a whim. When word reached him that the synagogue at Damascus was becoming inhabited with many followers of the Way, Paul received permission from the high priest Caiaphas to stamp out the threat.

As Paul reached the end of his 160-mile trip, hatred oozing out of every pore of his body, a great blazing light suddenly flashed around him, startling his horse and knocking Paul violently to the ground. His heart racing in fear and overwhelming dread, Paul heard a voice thundering from the very heavens. "Saul, Saul, why do you persecute me? It is hard for you to kick against the goads."[66]

---

[65] Acts 7:56

[66] Acts 26:14

How Paul was able to reply he had no idea, but the words managed to find their way out of him. "Who are you, Lord?" he stuttered.

"I am Jesus, whom you are persecuting. Now get up and stand on your feet!" Somehow, Paul managed to do it, though he could barely stand. The unrelenting voice resounded. "I have appeared to you to appoint you as a servant and as a witness of what you have seen of me and what I will show you. I will rescue you from your own people and from the Gentiles. I am sending you to them to open their eyes and turn them from darkness to light, and from the power of Satan to God, so that they may receive forgiveness of sins and a place among those who are sanctified by faith in me."[67]

Paul's life would never be the same. In an instant, the great hatred of his heart had been lifted. He had encountered the Christ, the One he had sought so hard to discredit and destroy. Instantly, a pervasive love inhabited his soul and permeated his entire being. He would spend the rest of his life proclaiming his uninhibited love for the Savior who had come to him so miraculously.

"And I pray that you, being rooted and established in love, may have power, together with all the saints, to grasp how wide and long and high and deep is the love of Christ."[68]

As Paul reflected back on his life of hatred, it seemed but a distant dream, a past reality that had died the moment he fell from his horse in that flash of glorious light.

---

[67] Acts 26:16–18
[68] Ephesians 3:17–18

"Oh, Lord," he cried out while falling to his knees, "what unfathomable love is this? And why would you call a man of hatred such as me to do your work? Oh, Lord, your love is too much for me to comprehend. What amazing, abundant love!"

Paul and You

Paul hated the early Church: "On the authority of the chief priests I put many of the saints in prison, and when they were put to death, I cast my vote against them" (Acts 26:10).

Now that's hatred.

What about you? Are you a believer in Christ who is consumed with hatred? If so, you need to overcome it.

Proverbs 10:12 says, "Hatred stirs up dissension, but love covers over all wrongs." If you are a person who harbors hatred, you are likely someone who causes dissension. How then can you obey this Bible teaching: "Make every effort to live in peace with all men and to be holy" (Hebrews 12:14)? A person filled with hatred is incapable of living in peace with others. Banish hatred and you banish dissension, enabling you to live in peace.

Also, notice how vile hatred in the believer is to God. Paul writes: "The acts of the sinful nature are obvious: sexual immorality, impurity and debauchery; idolatry and witchcraft; hatred, discord, jealousy, fits of rage, selfish ambition, dissensions, factions and envy; drunkenness, orgies, and the like" (Galatians 15:19–21). In case you think the hatred you harbor is a personal matter that harms no one, think again. See how hatred is placed smack-dab in the middle of the above list. It is mind-boggling to think that hatred rates right up there with sexual immorality, witchcraft, envy, and drunkenness. If you are prone to hatred, you are in this category. A sobering thought indeed!

If you are convicted about your hatred, your next step is to destroy it. But how?

Usually, hatred is directed at a person or persons. Jesus has this in mind when He says, "But I tell you: Love your enemies and pray for those who persecute you" (Matthew 5:44). Notice how Jesus says nothing here about your "enemies" asking you for forgiveness. You are to forgive them and pray for them no matter what. Such a selfless—and difficult—act will go a long way in dissipating your hatred.

The apostle Peter takes his Master one step further when he writes: "Above all, love each other deeply, because love covers over a multitude of sins" (1 Peter 4:8). Notice here, also, how there are no conditions attached to the command. You are to love, plain and simple. Not only are you to love, but you are to love "deeply." Love is the remedy for hatred.

But, you object, *I am not by nature a loving person. It is difficult for me to love unconditionally.*

There is but one answer: ask God the Father to endow you with this kind of love, for this is the only way you are ever going to attain it. Don't wait for God to knock you off your horse like He did with

Paul to get you to obey Him. Ask Him *now* to vanquish your deep-rooted hatred and replace it with blessed peace.

It may be the best request you ever make!

Mark

OVERCOMING COWARDICE

←❝❞→

John Mark could not help rereading the note. *Get Mark and bring him with you, because he is helpful to me in my ministry.* It had been sent by Timothy, Mark's fellow Christian worker. But more important was the one who had written the note.

"Ah, dear Paul," Mark said aloud, though no one was in the room with him, "you do not know how many times I have longed to read these words."

Paul, Mark knew, was wasting away in a Roman dungeon, and, according to his letter to Timothy, appeared to be close to death. He had asked both men to come to him, and Mark knew he *had* to go. He summoned a servant and told him to pack his clothes for him, because he would be leaving Jerusalem the next day for Rome. He would then have a different servant arrange transport for him to Caesarea Maritime, where he could book passage on a ship that would take him to Paul.

With it done, Mark was able to admire the note. He must have read it at least ten times before at last placing it on his table and leaning back. There was a time he thought he would never see such words.

He remembered back to his teenage years when everything he had ever believed was challenged to its core after he was introduced to the Rabbi from Nazareth, the man many were claiming was Israel's Messiah. He came to know Jesus at the end of His ministry, and was there when He was arrested. Like the others, however, he fled.

The next few astonishing days—punctuated by Jesus' trial, crucifixion, and resurrection—proved life-transforming as both he and his mother Miriam became firm believers in Jesus' Messiahship and deity.

They were among the early ones. A well-off widow with a large home, Miriam offered it to the new believers as a place for worship. Those were incredible days for young Mark as he got to meet those men and women who were closest to Jesus, the apostles James and John, as well as Jesus' own mother. But the man who most impressed Mark was the fisherman Peter, the one who freely confessed to failing Jesus by denying him three times. However, Peter was quick to add, "The Lord also redeemed me three times and has made me fit for service. I will be forever grateful."

And Mark was grateful for Peter, who came to love the young man and pour into him everything he learned from the great Master. With Peter's support, Mark became a champion of the early Jerusalem church.

Then about fifteen years following Christ's resurrection, Mark received the offer of a lifetime. "Dearest cousin," the letter began, "Paul, one of the great teachers of our faith, and I are embarking upon an extended mission where we will share the truth and grace of our Lord Jesus Christ with those who do not know Him. Paul and I greatly desire for you to join us. Please give us your answer soon. In Christ, Barnabas."

Mark was thrilled with the invitation, his mother sharing euphorically in this extraordinary opportunity.

The trio's first stop was the island of Cyprus, where they preached with amazing success in synagogues beginning in Salamis, a Greek city-state on the east side of the island. They continued scorching the souls of islanders, declaring the truth of Christ from one coast to another.

And then they came to Paphos, a seaside city on the island's southwest coast. All went well at first when they were greeted by the island's governor, Sergius Paulus. "You are welcome to Paphos," he said warmly. "Come to my home tomorrow for lunch and share your message. I have a great interest."

The next day found Paul, Barnabas, and Mark sufficiently wined and dined when Sergius said, "Anytime you wish to begin, Paul, I am ready to listen."

This was all the invitation Paul required. He spoke with a power, confidence, and conviction that had Sergius's guests riveted to Paul's every word. Everyone, that is, except for one dour-faced man whom

Mark could not take his eyes off. The man scowled at Paul the entire time he spoke, the hatred pouring out of him.

When Paul had finished after about an hour, Sergius was about to speak, but the man with the scowl, an adviser, intercepted him. "Certainly, sir, you are not swayed by such speech, are you?"

"What are you talking about, Elymas?" Sergius asked impatiently.

"Why, sir, the claims of this man…"

"Explain yourself."

"Surely, it must be obvious, sir. God as a man? Put to death? Then risen three days later? This is more a fantasy than truth, a fable of this man's imagination."

Again, Sergius was about to speak, but this time it was Paul who cut him off. "I could sense your venom from the moment I walked into this room, you sorcerer," he raged. "You are a child of the devil and an enemy of everything that is right! You are full of all kinds of deceit and trickery. Now the hand of the Lord is against you, and for a time you will be blind!"

Elymas immediately fell to the ground and began groping around for someone to help him. Sergius's shocked guests were stupefied, as was Mark. Many gave their lives to Christ that day—Sergius included. Mark, however, was deeply disturbed by the incident; this confrontation was beyond anything he had imagined. He was even more disturbed by the fact that the two older men were completely unfazed by what had happened.

Perhaps he was not qualified for this kind of work after all. He found himself longing for Jerusalem—for the sweet fellowship of the believers, for his mother, for the comfort of his home.

He made his wishes known to Paul, and the evangelist was furious, accusing Mark of being a deserter and a coward. Despite his peacemaking efforts, Barnabas could not prevent Mark from leaving, nor calm Paul's anger.

The next few years were torture for Mark, the guilt of his cowardice wreaking havoc on his conscience. He continued to serve the church but could not escape what he now regarded as an act of treachery. Had it not been for Peter's persistent encouragement, Mark may have fallen into total despair.

As the years passed, Mark slowly began to recover. He sat down with Peter on a crucial project: to write down the story of Jesus' three years of ministry. Drawing most of his firsthand accounts from Peter and with the enabling of the Holy Spirit, Mark was able to finish his book, the first Gospel on the life of Christ.

The accomplishment was a source of pride for Mark and offered a degree of redemption. He even heard from Peter that Paul had heard of the account and was proud of Mark for writing it. But, Mark wondered, was this just Peter trying to cheer him up? Then, about a year later, Mark was interrupted in his studies by a servant who told him that a guest was in the parlor waiting to see him. He did not give his name.

Mark entered the room, and when he reached it, he stopped dead in his tracks. "Greetings, Mark," the once-familiar voice said. "You look fit."

Mark could barely believe his eyes. Seeing Paul for the first time in over a decade left him totally flabbergasted. And mute.

"Surely, Mark, this silence of yours is out of character," Paul said with a smile. "From what I hear, you have become quite the speaker."

Mark gathered himself. "Forgive me, sir. You must know how honored I am to see you again. Your presence here is a balm to my soul."

"Balm?" Paul replied. "Do you seek healing, John Mark? If so, what for?"

"If healing is possible for a deserter and coward, then I seek healing."

Paul approached Mark and put his hand on his shoulder. "Deserter? Coward?" he said softly. "I see none in this room."

Mark was too overwhelmed to speak.

"To the point then, Mark," Paul said, backing up a few steps. "I am about to set off to Rome to bring the Gospel there. I will need the finest men I know. And that includes you. Mark, you have proven yourself a loyal and capable servant of our Lord Jesus. I want…need…you at my side. Tell me you will come with me."

Mark's tears were his reply.

The years with Paul were the most extraordinary of Mark's life. The triumphs were many, but so were the persecutions. Paul was imprisoned and Mark stayed with him, meeting his needs. Paul would eventually send Mark back to Jerusalem, where the great apostle felt Mark was more needed. But when Paul was imprisoned for the second time, he desperately sought Mark's company. And this time, Mark would not disappoint him.

His days of cowardice behind him, Mark could not wait to set out for Rome the following morning.

Mark and You

Mark suffered from a serious case of cowardice during his first missionary trip with Paul and Barnabas. Perhaps it was Paul's confrontation with the demon-possessed Elymas. Maybe it was the fact that the men were venturing deeper into Gentile territory. Perhaps Mark feared persecution, which could lead to his death. Whatever the reason, Mark was scared.

And you know what? So are you. We all are.

Though the Bible encourages us not to fear, the truth is that *all* Christians are fearful and act cowardly. Especially when it comes to sharing the Gospel. Why is this?

One reason is our fear of physical consequences. Sharing our faith often brings rejection and sometimes leads to your being spurned by friends and family. It could sometimes result in losing your job. In extreme cases—which occur daily in hostile nations— sharing one's faith often results in imprisonment, beatings, torture, and death.

However, the Bible would have you "transform" your thinking (Romans 12:2). Because you *know* you have eternal life if you believe in Jesus, death should be embraced rather than feared. Jesus said, "Do not be afraid of those who kill the body but cannot kill the soul. Rather, be afraid of the One who can destroy both soul and body in hell" (Matthew 10:28). The world can destroy your body, but once it does, you go immediately to paradise (Luke 23:43).

The apostle Paul says, "For you did not receive a spirit that makes you a slave again to fear, but you received the Spirit of sonship" (Romans 8:15). In other words, as God's adopted child, you are no longer subject to spiritual death. With this threat removed, all fear of death should evaporate with it. As Paul said elsewhere, "I am torn between the two: I desire to depart and be with Christ, *which is better by far*; but it is more necessary for you that I remain in the body" (Philippians 1:23–24, emphasis added). In other words, Paul actually prefers death (because it means eternity with Christ) than to go on living!

Despite these encouragements, living coward-free is tough. Paul understands this, which is why he writes to believers in Ephesus, "Pray also for me, that whenever I open my mouth, words may be given me so that I will *fearlessly* make known the mystery of the gospel, for which I am an ambassador in chains. Pray that I may declare it *fearlessly*, as I should" (Ephesians 6:19–20, emphasis added). Yep, even Paul prayed for courage! If he was not fearful, why would he ask *twice* for prayer that God would enable him to speak courageously?

Back in his day, Mark looked at his circumstances and fled in cowardly fear. Today, you look at the hostility you encounter from sharing your faith and do the same. But the Lord says, "Do not fear, for I am with you," (Isaiah 41:10).

And when you really think about it, that's all the reason you need to take courage!

The Philippian Jailer
OVERCOMING FEAR

←«»→

Julius[69] had never felt such fear.

His life would be over any second now, and by his own hand. As he aimed his sword at his heart, all he need do was make one swift plunge and it would be over. However, his trembling body would not guarantee a clean thrust, so he waited to calm his hand, at least enough to do what he needed to do. He could not risk missing his mark.

Julius thought about his family—his wife and three children. They would be mortified by the news of his death, but what choice did he have? Growing up in the Roman colony of Philippi, Julius began his professional career as a prison guard, but he eventually rose to the position of chief jailer—night shift. The promotion meant a better life for his family, a bigger home, and even a few slaves and servants.

Now, however, in a few short moments, every accomplishment he had ever worked for had come tumbling down as he found

---

[69] Character not named in the Bible. Name added to enrich story.

himself shaking in terror. That evening's shift had begun quietly, but it changed drastically within minutes of his arrival. He was in his quarters reviewing the records of the prisoners under his care when his second-in-command, Gaius, knocked at the door.

"Enter," Julius said, not looking up.

"Sir, I am afraid a matter has arisen that requires your attention. Two prisoners are heading our way and will soon be here. The magistrates want them watched carefully."

"Who are they, Gaius?"

"Two Jews: one named Paul; the other Silas."

"What have they done?"

"They are accused of causing a riot in the city."

Julius sat back and thought. "Two Jews, you say?"

"Yes, sir."

"I believe I know who you are speaking of, Gaius. Several times this week, as I have walked here, I would see these two men preaching. I never paid attention to them, except for one thing."

"What is that, sir?"

"That slave girl who predicts the future…do you know who I am speaking about?"

"I am familiar with her, sir."

"She would always be shouting, 'These men are servants of the Most High God, who are telling you the way to be saved.'" He paused. "What do you suppose she meant by that, Gaius?"

"I am not sure, sir."

Julius returned to the matter at hand. "What have these men done that they are to be watched so closely, Gaius?"

"Apparently, sir, the man named Paul turned to the girl and ordered her to be quiet. She had a spasm, fell to the ground, then rose again, unharmed."

"What of it?"

"It seems, sir, that these men caused the girl to lose her ability to predict the future. Her owners were furious and dragged the two Jews before the authorities. After hearing the case, they ordered the men to be severely flogged then brought here…"

A guard disrupted their briefing. "Sir, the two prisoners have arrived."

Julius rose. "I will see to this myself."

As he and Gaius made their way to the entrance of the prison, Julius saw the two men who had caused so much commotion. They were bleeding severely from their wounds but standing on their own.

"We will take them," Julius told the four guards assigned to them.

"We have been ordered by the magistrates to inform you that these men are to be given careful attention…"

"Yes," Julius interrupted, "I know. I will assume full responsibility from here."

The guards departed. Julius approached the two men and examined them. "You have caused quite a stir," he said to them.

They smiled kindly, which baffled Julius. "We are only doing the work of our God," one of the two men replied.

Julius looked at him closely and was struck by his placid countenance. "What is your name?"

"Paul. And this is my associate, Silas."

Julius looked closely at Paul. There was something definitely different about him. "These men look harmless, Gaius."

"I agree, sir, but we have been given orders."

Julius was still puzzled by their strange serenity. "Though it is against my better judgment, Gaius, I think it is best to place them in the inner cell and have their feet chained."

"Is this not a little extreme, sir?"

"It is, Gaius, but…"

Why these men had disturbed Julius, he had no idea, but he was at least satisfied that everything was under control. Returning to his quarters, Julius decided to lie down on his cot. He thought about the two new prisoners and what they had done to cause the magistrates to demand such caution. He eventually dozed off but awoke several hours later to the sound of singing. He rose to investigate and discovered that it was the two Jewish prisoners. They were singing and praying alternately, and Julius marveled at their tranquility. He was even more amazed that none of the other prisoners demanded their silence. They must have been as enthralled with these men as he was.

Julius felt a strange sense of peace as he returned to his cot around midnight and fell back to sleep. But not for long. Suddenly, he was again awakened, but not by singing. This time a savage shuddering was rocking the entire building. Julius was thrown to the ground as he heard a great commotion.

"Quick," he heard the guards shout while scurrying, "lock the cell doors!"

Julius turned white and bolted to the main cellblock. He was horrified! The cell doors were open—every one of them. Since only a mere bar secured them, it was an easy matter for an earthquake to shake them loose. Even more terrifying to Julius was the sound of clanging metal. Somehow, the chains of the inmates had come loose.

While the guards scrambled to recover escaped prisoners, Julius fell to his knees. He knew exactly what was happening. *Surely, every prisoner has fled*, he thought, terror consuming him. Just *one* escaped inmate required the death of the chief jailer, let alone multiple escapees. Julius knew that he faced a long, slow, and torturous execution. Trembling uncontrollably and sweating profusely, he drew his sword and pressed it against his chest.

However, so overcome by fear, he could not steady his hand. He would wait until he calmed down enough to thrust himself through. Now, resigned to death, he was ready to take his own life. But then…

"Wait!" a desperate voice pierced the darkness of his embittered soul. "Do not harm yourself! We are all here!"

The words cascaded upon him like waterfalls of solace. He quickly rose, called for Gaius to bring some torches, and raced to the cell of the two Jewish inmates where he again fell to his knees. "Sirs," he pleaded, "what must I do to be saved."

The man who replied—the one who urged him not to harm himself, the one called Paul—smiled and touched Julius's shoulder. "Believe on the Lord Jesus Christ, and you will be saved."

Julius was considering the incredible simplicity of the reply when a guard approached him. "Sir, all the prisoners are in their cells, and the doors have been secured. None has escaped."

Julius was mesmerized as he rose, still trembling. "Bring water and cloths so that I may wash these men's wounds."

The order was obeyed. "Sirs," Julius quivered, "what is this salvation you speak of?"

For the next half hour, Paul and Silas shared with Julius the good news about the Jewish prophet Jesus, who had been crucified but raised from the dead three days later. He was man's provision for sin and provided an escape from God's eternal wrath.

"Sirs," Julius pleaded, "you must come to my home and share this message with my household. My family, servants, and slaves need to hear these words."

Leaving Gaius in charge of the prison, Julius led Paul and Silas to his home just four blocks away. Though it was one o'clock in the morning, Julius ordered his entire household to rise and come to the dining hall. After feeding Paul and Silas, Julius implored them to share their message of salvation with those assembled.

As Paul and Silas spoke, Julius felt his soul well up with unimaginable peace. He looked around at the rapt faces and could tell that they, too, were feeling the same elation he had. And when Paul suggested that the entire household be baptized in the name of Jesus Christ in a pool of water on Julius's property, they immediately assented.

Julius was the first in the water. As he stepped his foot in the pool, he trembled, fear still lingering in his bones. As he sunk into the water, he felt its coolness wash over him, cleansing him from the great sins of his heathen past. As he rose to the surface and drew a deep breath, he felt the glory of salvation fill him in waves of joy and gratitude. As he rejoiced in the moment, he felt every fear that had ever tormented him vanquish in an instant, replaced by a new life, a wondrous existence.

A life, an existence, in which fear had no place.

The Philippian Jailer and You

Julius's fear was real.

He feared that his prisoners had escaped, and according to Roman law, a jailer who allowed a prisoner to escape was to pay with his life. Julius considered himself a dead man and was paralyzed with fear because of it.

What about you? Do you fear?

For most people, there are two primary causes of fear: *not being able to survive in this world* and *death*. To those who don't know Jesus Christ as their Lord and Savior, these are substantial fears. In the first instance, this world is all they know, so surviving in it means *everything*. Regarding death, the unbeliever has no idea where he or she is going, so fear of the unknown is intimately associated with the fear of death.

Not so for you if you are a believer. Regarding life in this world, Jesus says: "…do not worry, saying, 'What shall we eat?' or 'What shall we drink?' or 'What shall we wear?'…your heavenly Father knows that you need them" (Matthew 6:31–32). The apostle Paul says this: "And my God will meet all your needs according to His glorious riches in Christ Jesus" (Philippians 4:19). For the unbeliever, there is no provider; he is left to his own devices. However, for you, God is your Provider. He promises to meet *all* of your needs. Such assurance should remove all fear of survival.

"Easier said than done!" you object.

What if, suddenly, you became unable to afford to feed and nourish yourself? What if a deadly disease overtakes you? These things indeed elicit fear. The key is seeing through such dire circumstances and into the heart of the fear. It lies in having a proper view of death. John 5:24 tells you: "whoever hears My [Jesus'] word and believes Him who sent Me has eternal life and will *not* be condemned" (italic added). The condemnation referred to here is eternal separation from God in a place of torment (Revelation 20:14–15).

Contrary to eternal damnation, you as a Christian, upon death, will be ushered into God's eternal presence to a place referred to as "paradise" (Luke 23:43) and will eventually take your place in the "new heaven and…new earth" (Revelation 21:1). In that eternal place of blessing, you will live with God in the dwelling place that Jesus Himself will prepare for you (John 14:1–2).

So, what is your greatest fear? Is it being unable to survive in this world? God promises provision. Is it death and fear of the unknown? With death from this temporary world comes eternal paradise.

Until he came to know Christ, the Philippian jailer knew nothing but this world. After Christ, he knew the God of eternal blessing and lost all fear.

You, too, know God and are known by Him. So, whether your fears lie in this world or the next, they are unfounded. You are Christ's, and in Him all worldly fear is banished!

Timothy
OVERCOMING TIMIDITY

←«»→

Paul was dead and Timothy mourned. He would have to carry on alone, leading the church of Ephesus, a divided congregation stuck in the center of a city known for its religious perversion. "I cannot do this without Paul, Lord," Timothy lamented, then quickly stopped himself as Paul's written words suddenly streamed through his consciousness.

"For this reason I remind you to fan into flame the gift of God, which is in you through the laying on of my hands. For God did not give us a spirit of timidity, but a spirit of power, of love and of self-discipline."[70]

Timidity. It hounded Timothy all his life, and Paul urged him to rise above it. Paul knew that if his apprentice and partner in evangelism did not overcome his fear, he would be ineffective in carrying on Paul's work. And Timothy felt the weight of it. He was not a man of strong resolve or courage, and yet the great apostle had placed his hopes in him—as a father would his son. Yes, a son. That

---

[70] 2 Timothy 1:6–8

is exactly how Paul regarded Timothy—and, oh, how Paul's sweet words strengthened him now!

To the church at Corinth, Paul had written: "For this reason I am sending to you Timothy, my son whom I love, who is faithful in the Lord"[71] To the church at Philippi, he wrote: "But you know that Timothy has proved himself, because as a son with his father he has served with me in the work of the gospel."[72]

Those sweet endearments soothed Timothy's broken heart and settled his rattled nerves—the same nerves he felt when he saw Paul for the first time.

Timothy was a young man of sixteen and an active participant in the thriving synagogue of his hometown, Lystra. He was raised in Christian godliness by his grandmother Lois and mother Eunice. One Sabbath morning, Paul and his coworker Barnabas were to speak. The believers of Lystra had heard much about Paul, the one-time persecutor of the faith who, miraculously, had become its biggest champion. From the moment Paul began preaching, no one was disappointed. Timothy was enraptured by Paul's words—their power, their logic—and the confidence with which he delivered them.

Then, unexpectedly, Paul stopped. As Timothy, sitting toward the back, craned his head to discover what had halted Paul's dissertation, he noticed Paul staring at someone in the front row.

"Sir," Paul said to a man Timothy could not see. "What is your name?"

---

[71] 1 Corinthians 4:17
[72] Philippians 2:22

"Hiram, sir, and I have lived here all my life." Timothy knew the man well.

"How long have you been lame?" Paul asked.

"Since birth. I was born crippled and have never walked."

Paul then paused for just a moment. "Hiram," he said directly, "I can see your faith in your eyes. Indeed, you have faith to be healed."

Timothy felt his heart begin to race. "Hiram, in the name of Jesus Christ," Paul commanded, "be free of your affliction and stand on your feet!"

The synagogue emitted a collected gasp. Hiram leapt to his feet, as did Timothy and everyone else in the building. *What just happened?*

Timothy, not known for his aggression, found himself dashing to the front of the synagogue where Hiram was celebrating the miracle. Bedlam erupted as the unbelievers in the crowd began hailing Barnabas as Zeus—the god of sky and thunder; and Paul as Hermes—the great messenger of the gods. "The gods have come down to us in human form!" they shouted.

Some of the people rushed outside to the streets and began proclaiming this visitation of the gods. Horrified, Paul and Barnabas hurried to settle the frenzied mob. "We are but men!" they cried. No one listened.

The situation spiraled even more out of control when the priest of Zeus brought bulls and wreaths to offer sacrifices to Paul and Barnabas, who kept pleading for sanity. The crowd, however, would not be calmed.

Finally, a number of hostile Jewish men from nearby Antioch and Iconium who had been keeping close watch on Paul began to accuse the two evangelists of preaching false doctrine and of subverting Roman law. The fickle crowd soon turned on the two men and began stoning Paul, finally leaving him for dead.

As Timothy witnessed all this, he shrunk in fear, never having seen anything like it. As much as he wanted to, he felt powerless to help Paul. He was even more astonished when Paul made a full recovery just a few days later—and departed. However, he had left his mark on Timothy. The young man was determined to live for Christ as Paul had—if at all possible.

As the years passed, Timothy longed for the day when he would see Paul again. Six years later, that day came. Once again, Paul had come to speak in the synagogue of Lystra, but this time with a new companion, Silas. And just as he had done the first time, Timothy, now twenty-two, sat toward the back and was again enthralled by the great apostle's words. When Paul was finished, Timothy slowly made his way to the front, hoping to tell the great apostle how much he admired him.

As he approached, however, Timothy was thunderstruck when, suddenly, Paul looked directly at him and spoke. "Ah, Timothy," he said smiling, "I have been looking forward to meeting you."

Timothy was speechless. *How does he know who I am?*

Paul laughed. "I see I must speak for both of us."

Paul excused himself from the many well-wishers surrounding him and pulled Timothy aside. "Young man," Paul said softly,

"I have heard much about you." Timothy was baffled. His heart pounded. "The brothers in Iconium and here in Lystra have spoken well of you. Very well. I have never heard of any man as young as you elicit such praise."

Timothy could tell that Paul wanted him to respond, but he was unable. Paul laughed again. "Very well, then. I will get straight to it. The work of spreading the Gospel is difficult—physically and emotionally. To be honest, Timothy, I need help. I need the help of a young, strong man who knows the Word of God and loves the Lord with all his heart, soul, and mind. And, dear Timothy, from everything I hear—and convicted of by my prayers—I am convinced that you are that man. Will you join me in this sacred work?"

Timothy felt unsteady and somewhat dizzy. He never expected that this would be the outcome to his visit to the synagogue that day, but he knew exactly what he needed to do. Fighting for control of his soaring emotions, he gave Paul the only answer he could. "It would be my honor, sir, to serve you in any way you see fit. I will commit my life to the Lord and to you."

From that day forth, Timothy's very existence was transformed in ways he could never imagine as the two traveled the Near East and Rome and shared the Good News of Jesus Christ. It all culminated when Paul stunned Timothy by putting him in charge of the congregation at Ephesus.

"But, sir, I am too young to lead such an important congregation," Timothy objected when Paul broke the news. "Perhaps you can start me off in a small, rural town."

Paul smiled. "Do not let anyone look down on you because you are young," Paul said assuringly, putting his hand on Timothy's shoulder, "but set an example for the believers in speech, in life, in love, in faith and in purity. You can do this, my beloved son in the faith. I would not have assigned you to such a position had I not had the utmost confidence in you."

It was enough for Timothy, and, with Paul's unyielding support, he made it.

But now, after seventeen years together, Paul was dead. At age thirty-nine, Timothy felt unsure, alone, timid. "Oh, dear father, if only you could have stayed with me a few more years."

Then, in the depths of his soul, he suddenly remembered another charge by Paul. "My son, be strong in the grace that is in Christ Jesus. And the things you have heard me say in the presence of many witnesses entrust to reliable men who will also be qualified to teach others. Endure hardship with us like a good soldier of Christ Jesus."[73]

It then occurred to Timothy that these were not Paul's words at all, but God's. After all, Timothy well knew that Paul wrote by God's inspiration—the words God had given him to write. And if it was inspiration, then it was God Himself who was now leading Timothy.

Timothy fell to his knees. "I *will* endure as Your soldier, Lord Jesus. Thank you for my father Paul and all he did for me. But now, Lord, I live for You. Remove my fear. Banish my weakness. Conquer my timidity. Allow me to never fail you, Lord. Never."

---

[73] 2 Timothy 2:1–3

When he rose, Timothy was certain that Paul was smiling.

Timothy and You

Are you a Timothy? Are you timid and lack confidence? By timidity, the Bible is referring to areas related to the Gospel, specifically, the proclaiming of it.

In other words, do you love the Lord Jesus but fear speaking about Him to others? Does sharing your faith or standing up for Christ cause you to sweat and become tongue-tied? If so, Jesus lovingly says to you, "Take courage! It is I. Don't be afraid" (Matthew 14:27).

"That is easy for Him to say," you object. "After all, He is God."

True. However, Jesus would never tell you to do anything He knows you cannot do. And if He tells you to take courage, He will provide the courage you need. One reason you can overcome your timidity through Christ is that He "richly blesses all who call on him" (Romans 10:12). And if you are a timid person, this is entirely the point. God knows fully well what your nature is and He understands. His message to you is this: "I have called you to be mine, and I want you to serve Me. To do so, I will personally give you what you need in order to do what I call you to do."

In your situation, if it's courage you need, this is what God will give you—if You ask Him.

Here's a perfect example. Toward the end of His life, Jesus told His disciples—and *all* who would be His (you included)—that they will face hard times. However, no matter how bad things look, He never wants them to take their eyes off Him. Jesus says: "Whenever you are arrested and brought to trial, do not worry beforehand about what to say. Just say whatever is given you at the time, for it is not you speaking, but the Holy Spirit" (Mark 13:11).

In your situation, you may never be arrested for the Gospel, but you may be convicted by God to share the Truth with a family member, friend, neighbor, or coworker. Or there may be a time when you need to stand against those who are trying to discredit Christ. Don't let timidity stop you! Pray silently for God to help you form your words. Tell the Lord that you want to share His Truth with others, but that you can't do it alone. Tell Jesus to give you the words to say. And don't worry about being eloquent. So long as the Lord is leading you, the Holy Spirit will cause your words to be effective, powerful, and moving—despite your timidity!

So, are you a timid person? Guess what? So was Timothy, and he was put in charge of one the most important churches of his day. What does God have in store for you? Do you want to find out? Then overcome your timidity, get down on your knees, and ask God for the courage to do great things for Him!

There is nothing timid about that!

Since 1990 David Ettinger has written for the magazine *Zion's Fire*, published by Zion's Hope, a faith mission that seeks to graciously proclaim to the Jewish people their need for personal salvation through Jesus the Messiah, and to proclaim the Gospel of the Lord Jesus Christ to all men regardless of race, religion, gender, education, or national origin.

For more information about Zion's Hope or for a one-year gift-subscription to *Zion's Fire*, please:

- Call 1-888-781-9466
- E-mail *info@zionshope.org*
- Visit *www.zionshope.org*
- Write to them at P.O. Box 783369, Winter Garden, FL 34778

To read more articles by David Ettinger, please visit his website at *www.ettingerwriting.com*.

Made in the USA
Columbia, SC
14 February 2024